"Clay Routledge makes the thought-provoking case that looking back with nostalgia can actually be good for us. *Past Forward* comes to a surprising but solid conclusion: thinking about the past can help us cope, build self-esteem, connect to others, and manage stress. It's a fascinating look into the research on how humans think about time."

JEAN M. TWENGE, PHD
author of *Generations*

"In *Past Forward*, acclaimed psychologist Clay Routledge delves deeply into the profound and often underestimated power of nostalgia. Drawing on decades of research, this thought-provoking and lucidly written book unravels the mysteries of our longing for the past and reveals how we can all use nostalgia intentionally to improve our present lives and build a brighter future."

CONSTANTINE SEDIKIDES, PHD
professor of social psychology, University of Southampton, UK

"If you miss 'the good old days,' well, lucky you. In *Past Forward*, Clay Routledge shows us that nostalgia is an unmistakably positive force in life—combating loneliness, boosting self-esteem, and driving society forward. A fascinating book."

ARTHUR C. BROOKS, PHD
professor at the Harvard Kennedy School and Harvard Business School, author of *From Strength to Strength*, a #1 *New York Times* bestseller

"In *Past Forward*, Clay Routledge convincingly argues that nostalgia can be a critical ally of progress. Counterintuitively, our nostalgic longing for the past doesn't hold us back. It helps us adapt to a changing world and find the motivation to move forward with an optimistic outlook. Importantly, Routledge shows readers how they can take advantage of the power of nostalgia to improve their own lives and the world around them."

MARIAN L. TUPY
founder and editor of humanprogress.org, coauthor of *Ten Global Trends Every Smart Person Should Know* and *Superabundance*

"Clay Routledge thoughtfully explores the value of memories and nostalgia, emphasizing their profound impact on our personal growth and collective advancement, urging us to embrace the past as a guiding force toward a brighter tomorrow. For our scrapbooking community, we've known for a long time that there is magic in nostalgia, but Clay Routledge helps us understand exactly how that magic of the past impacts our futures."

ALISON DUTTON
CEO of Creative Memories

PAST
FORWARD

Also by Clay Routledge

Supernatural: Death, Meaning, and the
Power of the Invisible World

HOW NOSTALGIA CAN HELP YOU LIVE A MORE MEANINGFUL LIFE

PAST FORWARD

CLAY ROUTLEDGE, PHD

sounds true
BOULDER, COLORADO

Sounds True
Boulder, CO

Published 2023

Cover design by Huma Ahktar
Book design by Meredith Jarrett

Printed in the United States of America

BK06313

Library of Congress Cataloging-in-Publication Data

Names: Routledge, Clay, author.
Title: Past forward : how nostalgia can help you live a more meaningful
   life / Clay Routledge, PhD.
Description: Boulder, CO : Sounds True, Inc., 2023. |
   Includes bibliographical references.
Identifiers: LCCN 2023016948 (print) | LCCN 2023016949 (ebook) |
   ISBN 9781683648642 (paperback) | ISBN 9781683648659 (ebook)
Subjects: LCSH: Nostalgia. | Quality of life.
Classification: LCC BF575.N6 R69 2023 (print) | LCC BF575.
N6 (ebook) |
   DDC 152.4--dc23/eng/20230808
LC record available at https://lccn.loc.gov/2023016948
LC ebook record available at https://lccn.loc.gov/2023016949

10 9 8 7 6 5 4 3 2 1

CONTENTS

Part 5: Using the Past to Build a Better Future

INTRODUCTION

> You must know that there is nothing higher and stronger and
> more wholesome and good for life in the future than some good
> memory, especially a memory of childhood, of home. People talk
> to you a great deal about your education, but some good, sacred
> memory, preserved from childhood, is perhaps the best education. If
> a man carries many such memories with him into life, he is safe to
> the end of his days, and if one has only one good memory left in
> one's heart, even that may sometime be the means of saving us.
>
> **FYODOR DOSTOEVSKY, *THE BROTHERS KARAMAZOV*[1]**

At our core, humans are a progress-oriented species. We aren't satisfied with the world our ancestors left us. We strive to make it better. Culture plays a role, of course. In some parts of the world, people live much as they have for several generations; in others, societies change dramatically within a single lifetime. My grandmother rode a horse to her small country school as a child, and she watched the first moon landing on television as an adult.

Even in the United States—a relatively young nation that prides itself on being a forward-looking and dynamic society—there are subcultures such as the Amish that purposely reject features of modernity to preserve an older way of life.

Though cultures differ in the extent to which they prioritize change or stability, at some fundamental level, humans are equipped with psychological characteristics that push us toward novelty seeking, exploration, creativity, invention, innovation, and future-oriented goals aimed at improving the world for ourselves and our descendants.

Even the Amish and other groups that appear to be anti-progress don't entirely reject modern technological innovations. They are just more cautious and deliberate about how they approach change. The Amish studies professor Donald Kraybill at Elizabethtown College has spent decades studying the Amish and has documented ways the Amish navigate technological progress. For example, some Amish people have started using cellular phones to improve their ability to communicate for work or with people in other Amish communities that are far away. Additionally, Amish entrepreneurs and businesses will sometimes use electricity and power tools to compete with modern businesses. What is key to the Amish when deciding what technology is acceptable to use is whether it will potentially undermine or support community bonds and traditions. For example, televisions, radios, and personal computers are largely avoided out of concern that they will threaten the Amish way of life by introducing foreign cultural messages through mass media.[2]

The Amish creatively modify technology in ways that allow them to take advantage of progress without letting it compromise their cultural beliefs. For example, Amish communities don't want to rely on the electric grid as this would increase their dependence on the outside world. For this reason, they have experimented with ways of using air pressure, batteries, and other sources of power so that they can use some modern appliances.

Many efforts to restore an older way of living actually reflect a desire for progress. An urban dweller who wants to move toward a simpler way of living that is more connected to nature may look to new models of remote work made possible by advances in computer technology as well as new ideas about organizational structure and management. Someone like this isn't looking to abandon modern professional and economic life to live off the land, nor are they longing for the physically challenging and dangerous existence of early American frontier life. They have a contemporary vision of interacting with nature. They seek a lifestyle that will allow them to gain the physical and mental health benefits of a slower pace of life in the country while benefiting from emerging technology, changing business culture, and the latest discoveries about health and wellness.

Most people don't want to live exactly like their ancestors did; they want to use the past as inspiration for improving their lives. They are borrowing from the past to build a better future. Understanding this point helps us understand the power of nostalgia.

We are a progress-oriented species, but we are also a nostalgic species. As much as we are driven to plot out paths for our future, we feel the pull of our past. This tendency isn't a barrier to progress. The past paves the way for a better future. Just as the lessons of history are critical to progress, personal and collective memories offer valuable guidance for the decisions we need to make going forward. Our nostalgia works hand in glove with our hopes and dreams for the future.

At first blush, nostalgia may seem to conflict with progress. After all, our longing for yesteryear is often accompanied with a displeasure with the present and fears about the future. If our response to present-day problems and future challenges is to feel nostalgic for the past, wouldn't that make nostalgia an enemy of progress? Even if nostalgia gives us a warm, fuzzy feeling, might it ultimately get in the way of us improving our lives and making a positive difference in the world?

My hope is that after reading this book, you won't think of nostalgia as a barrier to personal growth and societal progress. Instead, you will appreciate nostalgia as a critical ingredient of personal growth and societal progress.

As you will learn, nostalgia has a fairly wild history. It was once considered by experts to be a medical disease and mental illness, but modern psychological science is discovering that nostalgia is a psychological resource that helps us in various ways. If we want to better understand and find inspiration from our true selves, connect with and serve others, live a meaningful and intentional life, and improve our communities and the broader world, we should embrace nostalgia, not reject it.

Nostalgia doesn't get in the way of building a better future for ourselves and others. Nostalgia inspires personal growth, social and community engagement, and human progress and flourishing. When we engage in nostalgia, we are not moving toward the past. We are bringing the past to the present to help us plan for the future. Nostalgia pushes us forward, not back.

PART 1

THE NOSTALGIA REVOLUTION

CHAPTER 1

THE NEW SCIENCE OF NOSTALGIA

My personal path to studying nostalgia began when I was an undergraduate student and started thinking seriously about how humans experience time. I have always been a fan of science-fiction movies about time travel. I'm not alone. People love thinking about what life was like in the past and what it might look like in the future.

For my first lab experiment on the subject, I designed and ran a study to figure out if time feels different when people listen to pleasant or unpleasant sounds. I found that the same amount of time feels longer if you are listening to unpleasant sounds (not a shocking discovery, I know). I probably made plenty of mistakes during this early study, but the experience of exploring ways to scientifically investigate how the human mind works (along with some encouragement from a few inspiring professors) helped me realize that I wanted to pursue psychological research as a career.

Later, as a psychology grad student, I remained fascinated with the psychology of time and how so much of human mental life involves thinking about time. We use our imagination to engage both the past and the future, and we don't just do it for pleasure. Sure, we enjoy imagining the lives of people living in ancient Rome, the Wild West of America, and even other worlds in distant futures when humans are able to travel through space like they do in *Star Trek*. But our capacity for mental time travel is also functional; it helps us learn and grow. It also helps us cope with challenges and stressors we face in the present.

Turns out I was not the only psychologist fascinated by mental time travel. Thousands of miles away in England, two social psychologists who would later become my colleagues and good friends were also thinking about time but more specifically about people's sentimental feelings about their own past. Constantine Sedikides and Tim Wildschut at the University of Southampton were launching a new research project focused on developing a science of nostalgia, while my PhD advisor, Jamie Arndt, and I were developing our own nostalgia project at the University of Missouri. Once both research teams learned about each other, we decided to combine our efforts and collaborate.

> Nostalgia is a ubiquitous, crucial, and rewarding aspect of the human experience.

As we would later learn, most people regularly experience nostalgia. Even those of us who study nostalgia for a living are not immune to its pull. Nostalgia is a ubiquitous, crucial, and rewarding aspect of the human experience.

Nostalgia's Complicated Past

Based on hundreds of studies conducted over the last two decades, this book makes the case that nostalgia improves our lives. This evidence-based view of nostalgia stands in stark contrast to how scholars and medical professionals thought about nostalgia for centuries. Until our team and a few other contemporary scholars started systematically examining how nostalgia works, the generally accepted view among scholars, mental health practitioners, and other thought leaders was that nostalgia is detrimental. The view dates all the way back to when the word *nostalgia* was first coined by Johannes Hofer, a Swiss medical student, in 1688.

Hofer created the term to indicate what he believed to be a medical illness among Swiss mercenary soldiers who were serving in European wars far from home. *Nostalgia* is the combination of two Greek words: *nostos* (return to the native land) and *algos* (pain). In other words, nostalgia was originally thought of as the pain caused by the desire to return to one's native land.

Hofer proposed that nostalgia was causing these soldiers a significant amount of psychological and physical distress. These men not only complained of constantly longing for home but they also experienced sadness, anxiety, fatigue, insomnia, irregular heartbeat, loss of appetite and thirst, indigestion, fevers, and related symptoms. Some of them were so distressed that they had to be discharged from military service. Ultimately Hofer viewed this condition as a neurological disorder that was caused by "the quite continuous vibrations of animal spirits through those fibers of the middle brain in which impressed traces of ideas of the Fatherland still cling."[1]

Hofer's view of nostalgia as a disease would become shared by other physicians of the time. But there was disagreement as to what caused this ailment. One fellow doctor proposed that nostalgia was caused by "a sharp differential in atmospheric pressure causing excessive body pressurization, which in turn drove blood from the heart to the brain, thereby producing the observed affliction of sentiment," believing this account explained why nostalgia was afflicting Swiss soldiers fighting in regions with a much lower altitude than their homeland.[2] Based on the idea that nostalgia was a Swiss disease, some physicians even suggested that it was caused by clanging of cowbells in the Alps, which might be responsible for trauma to the eardrum and brain.

Nostalgia would be viewed as a disease of the brain or medical illness well into the nineteenth century, but the illness wasn't confined to the Swiss. Nostalgia was documented among British, French, and German soldiers. During the American Civil War, Union physicians reported that many Northern soldiers fighting in Southern states required treatment for this disease. Some scholars proposed that nostalgia was not a uniquely human disease and that perhaps dogs, cats, horses, and cows could come down with it as well. It's no surprise that nostalgia would become a global illness because the homesickness that was believed to be at its core was not specific to any one group of people. But eventually the view that nostalgia was a disease started to fall out of favor as physicians failed to find any link between nostalgia and bodily processes.

It's worth noting that a few scholars challenged the mainstream view of nostalgia by observing that the longing for the past often involved positive emotions. For example, Charles Darwin, when describing people's recollections on the past, wrote, "The feelings which are called tender are difficult to analyze; they seem to be compounded of affection, joy, and especially of sympathy. These feelings are in themselves of a pleasurable nature, excepting when pity is too deep, or horror is aroused, as in hearing of a tortured man or animal."[3] However, for the most part, nostalgia was still viewed as a negative experience.

With the rise of psychology in the early twentieth century came a new way of framing nostalgia as a sickness, but this time a mental one. Some psychologists saw nostalgia as a form of depression and entertained ideas such as nostalgia representing stunted mental growth arising from a failure to let go of childhood, or nostalgia reflecting a subconscious desire to return to one's fetal state. In other words, nostalgia was still a problem—a problem of the mind as opposed to one of the body.

During this time, there was another change in how experts thought about nostalgia. Originally nostalgia was tied to homesickness. To suffer from nostalgia meant to be separated from one's home and long to return. But during the twentieth century, psychologists began recognizing that just as people could attach their longing for the past to a specific place—home—they could also attach it to a range of objects, people, and even abstract aspects of the past. For instance, someone can long for the days of their youth when they felt freer. This feeling might involve places (missing home), but it could also reflect missing people, hobbies, the structure (or lack of structure) of daily life, and one's previous state of mind.

At this point, nostalgia and the concept of homesickness started to become differentiated. Scholars and practitioners who were focused on the anxiety and related emotional states associated with separation from home began building a narrower area of research on homesickness. This paved the way for a broader analysis of people's more general nostalgic longing for various aspects of their past. Whereas homesickness is clearly tied to psychological distress, nostalgia was beginning to be understood as something more emotionally complex.

Psychologists started to see that yearning for the past has a positive emotional dimension. It isn't solely about the pain of something or someone that isn't present. It's also about the pleasant feelings that come to mind when thinking about those past experiences and people. Once this deeper and more complex understanding of nostalgia as pleasure mixed with pain began to emerge, the view of nostalgia as a mental illness started to fall out of favor.

> Nostalgia helps people make sense of their lives.

It was then that scholars and practitioners began to imagine the upside of nostalgia. If nostalgia was an experience that could generate positive emotions, then perhaps it had psychological value. In 1979, the sociologist Fred Davis published a book on the sociology of nostalgia in which he proposed that nostalgia helped people cope with major life changes by "encouraging an appreciative stance toward former selves; excluding unpleasant memories; reinterpreting 'marginal, fugitive, and eccentric facets of earlier selves' in a positive light; and establishing benchmarks of one's biography."[4] In other words, nostalgia helps people make sense of their lives. Later in the book I'll describe research that supports the idea that nostalgia helps us create and maintain a continuous self-story.

Clinical psychologists were also beginning to entertain therapeutic benefits of nostalgia. Some proposed that older adults suffering from dementia could benefit from nostalgic reminiscence, that it might help them restore or maintain a sense of identity—a possibility that recently has gained scientific support. Nostalgia was also proposed as a resource that might help people deal with loss and trauma—another idea that is now supported with scientific research.

Even though nostalgia's reputation was changing among psychologists and other academics, there was still little actual scholarly research on the topic, and the potential mental health benefits of nostalgia were largely speculative. To truly understand how people experience nostalgia and what it does to help or harm them, systematic scientific work was needed.

Nostalgia in the Age of Marketing

Quantitative approaches to studying nostalgia first occurred in the field of marketing and consumer psychology. These researchers observed that throughout people's lives, they are especially attracted to products and media they consumed in their late teens and early twenties. For example, studies show that people like music that was popular in their teens and early twenties more than music that was popular before or after that time in their lives. The same goes for favorite movie stars, films, and automobile models (especially for men).

> Think about your own consumer choices and habits. Do you feel that music today isn't as good as music from your youth? Do you wonder why they quit making such good movies? When you look back and have a laugh at some of the ridiculous fashion choices you made as a teen, is there a part of you that favors the styles of that time?

Even if you like new music, movies, and fashions, most people remain biased toward pop cultural trends from their youth. Modern internet streaming music and movie companies are well aware of this, which is why you can find old TV shows, movies, and music albums using these digital services.

Such research further casts doubt on the idea that nostalgia is a form of mental distress. Many people clearly have positive feelings about experiences from their youth and will spend their time and money in ways that allow them to revisit specific periods of their lives, even if they do so in ways that bring a modern touch.

In fact, several film franchises and television programs were explicitly created to serve the nostalgia market, combining nostalgia with the technological progress that improves the viewing experience. New *Star Wars* movies and shows revisit old characters but have the benefit of improved special effects, for example. Of course, they also introduce new characters and story lines, but connecting new material to people's nostalgia for past characters and narratives is a crucial part of the recipe for big profits. Though companies such as Disney create new franchises, their overall success relies heavily on the continuation of stories and characters that hooked people decades ago.

Not to mention that a considerable amount of advertising uses nostalgia to encourage people to desire and ultimately purchase a product. And it works. Studies find that advertisements that induce nostalgia increase positive attitudes toward brands and intentions in consumers to purchase those brands. Research also finds that using nostalgia to advertise a product increases how much attention people pay to the ad as well as how favorably they view the ad and the brand being advertised. These days, retro-marketing is a huge deal.

Studies that examine how nostalgia influences consumer decision-making and how marketers use nostalgia to sell products help us better understand the role that nostalgia plays in human decision-making. They reveal that nostalgia entails emotionally pleasing qualities and motivational power. People appear to enjoy buying things that take them back to the good old days. But these studies give us little detail about what goes on inside people's minds when they experience nostalgia, and they don't answer broader questions about why people experience nostalgia in the first place or how nostalgia ultimately impacts well-being.

From the late 1600s to the late 1900s, nostalgia went from being thought of as a horrible and even life-threatening brain disease to a major source of pleasure and entertainment that has likely generated billions in revenue for companies large and small. And yet at the beginning of the twenty-first century, little was known about the psychology of nostalgia. Using the tools of modern behavioral science, psychologists were studying various dimensions of human mental life, but they weren't studying nostalgia. That would soon change. And I had the privilege of being one of the researchers pioneering this new field within psychological science.

The Modern Science of Nostalgia

In the first two decades of this new century, the science of nostalgia has exploded. There are now hundreds of published scientific studies exploring a wide range of questions about how humans experience nostalgia and the different roles it plays in daily life. Scholars from all over the world are now conducting diverse studies about the ways nostalgia influences our lives.

Keeping in mind the history of nostalgia, it's amazing what we are now learning. Nostalgia is certainly not a disease and it's far more than just a source of entertainment. By using the gold standard of science— experiments in which research participants are randomly assigned to different treatment conditions—we've been able to answer a number of key questions. What causes people to experience nostalgia? How does nostalgia impact how people feel about their current lives? Does nostalgia influence our interests, goals, and behavior? If so, in what ways? Do the effects of nostalgia differ from person to person?

Nostalgia lifts our spirits and offers stability and guidance when life becomes chaotic and the future feels uncertain.

In addition to experimental studies, we have now conducted rigorous survey studies observing how nostalgia naturally occurs and what psychological characteristics, life experiences, and behaviors it tends to be associated with. This has helped us answer other intriguing questions. Are some individuals naturally more nostalgic than others? Is there a nostalgic personality type? Are people more or less nostalgic at different ages? Are people more or less nostalgic when experiencing different life changes such as moving away from home, starting a new career, facing personal tragedy and loss, or experiencing major life disruptions such as a global pandemic?

Over the last two decades, we have asked thousands of people to document their nostalgic memories. This has given us a great deal of insight into the more qualitative experience of nostalgia, which has in turn helped us develop a more complete picture of what happens inside a person's mind when they take a nostalgic trip down memory lane. These personal stories have guided a lot of my research questions on the topic.

Combining these different approaches to researching nostalgia, my colleagues and I have made a number of discoveries that cast this old emotional experience in a brand-new light. We've put nostalgia under the microscope, and what we've discovered is that nostalgia doesn't cause problems as proposed by past scholars, physicians, and psychologists. On the contrary, problems cause nostalgia.

When people are down because they feel sad, lonely, meaningless, uncertain, or even just bored, they often turn to nostalgia. Nostalgia lifts our spirits and offers stability and guidance when life becomes chaotic and the future feels uncertain. Even though nostalgia contains sentiments of loss, it ultimately makes people feel happier, more authentic and self-confident, more loved and supported, and more likely to perceive life as meaningful. In addition, nostalgia inspires action. Nostalgia starts with people self-reflecting on cherished memories, but it also drives people to look outside of themselves, help others, create, and innovate.

Though I've been researching nostalgia for a couple of decades now, I've remained excited about the topic because there is still so much to learn and so many ways to apply the knowledge we've gained to helping people improve their lives and the world we all share.

Get out a pen or pencil and a piece of paper; or use a digital device, such as a phone, tablet, or computer. Briefly jot down your reactions to the following questions: How would you define nostalgia? Do you consider yourself to be highly nostalgic, moderately nostalgic, or rarely nostalgic? Do you think the activities in which you engage in the present—from your work to your personal hobbies—are meaningfully influenced by nostalgia? Do you think nostalgia can help you pursue your current goals and make plans for the future? Finally, what is a nostalgic memory that really stands out as special to you? Describe this memory and how it makes you feel. Then revisit these questions and this memory once you've completed reading this book.

Summary Notes for "The New Science of Nostalgia"

- Johannes Hofer coined the term nostalgia in 1688 to describe a neurological illness in Swiss soldiers. Nostalgia was considered a disease of the brain or medical illness well into the nineteenth century.

- In the early twentieth century, psychologists began framing nostalgia as a sickness not of the body but of the mind.

- Eventually psychologists acknowledged that nostalgia had a positive emotional dimension that could generate positive emotions and help people make sense of their lives.

- The fields of marketing and consumer psychology were the first to engage in quantitative approaches to studying nostalgia, which helps explain why advertising has long employed nostalgia to get people to buy certain products.

- Hundreds of scientific studies on nostalgia reveal that nostalgia doesn't cause problems; problems cause nostalgia.

- Nostalgia improves our moods, offers stability and guidance when life gets rough, and makes us feel happier, more connected, and more inspired to action.

CHAPTER 2

NOSTALGIA IS ABOUT THE FUTURE

Despite what most people think, nostalgia isn't really about the past. It's about the future. More specifically, nostalgia is about building a better future.

I know this sounds absurd, and you should certainly be skeptical of this bold claim. How could nostalgia be about the future given that it's an experience that is so obviously focused on returning to bygone days? And how could nostalgia be about building a better future given that it involves a longing for yesteryear?

I frequently witness social commentators, business analysts, and mental health professionals warn people that nostalgia is harmful to individuals and society. To them, nostalgia represents a mindset that gets in the way of fully living in the present and planning for the future. They imagine nostalgia as an unhealthy indulgence or an attempt to hide from or even deny the existence of present-day challenges. Some even think of nostalgia as an intellectual shortcoming or emotional immaturity that results from a resistance to change.

Others have a less negative view of nostalgia but still see it as a vulnerability. They don't believe nostalgia has any real value. To them, nostalgia is a waste of time, even if people get some enjoyment out of it. Nostalgia is like reading a trashy novel or playing a mindless video game—a hedonistic experience that does nothing to help you grow as a person.

As I discussed in chapter 1, there's a long history of nostalgia being treated as a human weakness. Present-day critics of nostalgia aren't the first to argue that nostalgia is harmful or a barrier to healthy living and personal growth.

But both past and present-day nostalgia critics are wrong. Like other activities that are good for your health (such as physical exercise), you can definitely overdo it with nostalgia. But most people don't overdo it, just as most people don't work out too much.

If anything, people don't fully appreciate the power of nostalgia and thus don't use it to its fullest potential. Just like physical exercise, nostalgia can be used to improve your life. And that's just the beginning. The benefits of nostalgia extend far beyond the individual. Nostalgia helps people connect with others and inspires the types of aspirations that lead to human progress and flourishing.

In this book I argue that nostalgia is a future-oriented experience that, importantly, can be employed to make your life, the lives of those around you, and the broader world better. My view of nostalgia is not based on speculation or some gut feeling. It's based on twenty years of conducting scientific research on the psychology of nostalgia in which I and many other social and behavioral scientists have studied nostalgia's causes, the ways in which people from all over the world experience nostalgia, and how nostalgia affects people's feelings, attitudes, goals, and behaviors. I've also helped a number of organizations use nostalgia to improve people's lives.

What Is Nostalgia?

If you look up the definition of nostalgia on the internet, the first thing you might come across is something like "a sentimental longing or wistful affection for the past, typically for a period or place with happy personal associations." According to *Collins English Dictionary*, nostalgia is "a wistful desire to return in thought or in fact to a former time in one's life, to one's home or homeland, or to one's family and friends; a sentimental yearning for the happiness of a former place or time."[1] The *Cambridge Dictionary* describes nostalgia as "a feeling of pleasure and also slight sadness when you think about things that happened in the past."[2] Other dictionaries offer similar definitions that emphasize a longing for the past and one associated with both pleasure and pain.

Dictionary definitions are useful but don't always reveal how we think about a concept. What does nostalgia mean to everyday people? Turns out most people share an understanding of nostalgia even if they don't know the technical definition. This isn't just the case in the United States or other Western nations. People around the world of different languages and cultures think about and experience nostalgia much the same.

In one study, a large international research team led by Erica Hepper, a psychology professor at the University of Surrey in the United Kingdom, and Tim Wildschut and Constantine Sedikides, psychology professors at the University of Southampton in the United Kingdom, examined the extent to which individuals across eighteen different nations representing diverse cultures and societies agree or disagree on how they describe nostalgia.[3] These nations included Australia, Cameroon, Chile, China, Ethiopia, Germany, Greece, India, Ireland, Israel, Japan, Netherlands, Poland, Romania, Turkey, Uganda, the United Kingdom, and the United States. The researchers found strong agreement across countries. People all over the world view nostalgia as a past-oriented experience focused on cherished memories, often associated with childhood and youth, though people's nostalgic experiences can come from any time in their lives. In addition, they agree that nostalgia is typically social in nature and that it frequently features close relationships.

> The emotional and cognitive complexity of nostalgia helps make it a source of inspiration and hope.

People all over the world also share an understanding of the emotional complexity of nostalgia. Universally, people associate nostalgia more with positive feelings such as happiness than with negative feelings. Importantly, they also associate nostalgia with a sense of longing, loss, and even a desire to return to the past. In other words, nostalgia is understood as a primarily positive but also somewhat bittersweet emotional experience.

This emotional cocktail of positive feelings mixed with a dash of the bittersweet is part of what distinguishes nostalgia from other psychological states and part of what makes nostalgia such a powerful experience. People can have emotionally positive memories that don't make them nostalgic or generate the benefits of nostalgia.

In other words, nostalgia is more than just a happy memory. Life is full of pleasant experiences that we don't feel nostalgic about. The emotional and cognitive complexity of nostalgia helps make it a source of inspiration and hope, and a guiding light for reorienting ourselves toward the experiences, aspirations, and people that make life meaningful.

For example, in one of the many studies I've conducted, a research participant described feeling nostalgic for her childhood summers spent with her grandmother. This nostalgia involved all sorts of happy memories. Thinking back on this time, this participant felt the same love and joy she experienced when she was with her grandmother. But she also felt sad, because those days were long gone and her grandmother was no longer alive. Importantly, these complex feelings came together to generate feelings of inspiration and hope. The woman indicated that those nostalgic memories made her want to create similar memories for her future grandchildren and more broadly to want to help others experience the love and joy she'd felt under the care of her grandmother. Nostalgia reminded her that you never know how long you have with loved ones and that it's best not to take that time for granted. Ultimately this woman's nostalgia made her grateful, and it motivated her to act with purpose.

Think about a nostalgic memory that involves both positive and negative feelings and makes you feel grateful. How do the negative feelings connect to the positive ones to help you experience gratitude?

Why Nostalgia Is about the Future

Although I've been conducting scientific research on the psychology of nostalgia for over twenty years, it's only in the last several years that the lightbulb went off in my head about nostalgia's relationship with the future. Sure, nostalgia takes us back to the good old days. But a deeper inspection reveals that this trip to the past is really about packing a bag for a journey into the future. The past isn't the true destination; it's just where we go to grab supplies for the trip.

Since the early 2000s, I've been conducting studies with an international team of research psychologists in which we measure how people feel after they experience nostalgia (more details on that work later). The punch line of those studies is that nostalgia generally makes people feel good. After spending a few minutes writing about a nostalgic memory or listening to music that induces nostalgia, people tend to feel happier and more connected to loved ones, and they experience a greater sense of meaning in life. These are just a few of the many positive emotional states that nostalgia provokes.

Even after years of documenting these psychological benefits, I didn't truly understand what nostalgia was doing for people. I knew that the original view of nostalgia as a neurological disease was way off base, but I was only seeing part of the picture. I viewed nostalgia as useful, but more along the lines of a psychological defense—I thought of nostalgia as a way that people could counter negative feelings with more positive ones. In other words, I thought of nostalgia as a way to fight back against negative emotions to restore people to baseline. When people experience distressing mental states such as anxiety, fear, loneliness, sadness, and so on, they retreat to the past as a way to reduce the pains and sorrows of the present.

That's definitely part of the story. My colleagues and I (as well as other researchers) have conducted many studies that show that when people experience unpleasant emotional states, they tend to become more nostalgic—and nostalgia makes people feel better. So, from this perspective, nostalgia can be thought of as a psychological defense mechanism that we turn to when life gets difficult. But there's so much more to the story.

Turns out, nostalgia doesn't just make us feel better in the present. It puts us on the path to a more fulfilling future. I will expand this idea throughout the book, but here is an example of how this works in relationships: People often feel nostalgic when they are lonely or isolated. This is because nostalgia is social in nature; our nostalgic memories almost always feature family, friends, or other significant relationships. Even nostalgic memories that seem self-focused (such as those involving a major personal accomplishment) tend to involve an appreciation for other people. For example, in one study I conducted, a research participant described having nostalgic memories about being a very good tennis player in high school. His nostalgic reflection highlighted his dedication to training and victories on the court, but these memories about his individual success always included important relationships with his team, coach, and supportive parents.

So, when we are disconnected and long for social contact, our minds naturally wander toward the past times when we experienced connection—especially connection in which we felt valued and supported by close others.

During the COVID-19 pandemic, my wife and I had this experience a number of times. We would talk about road trips we'd taken to visit family members or times when we'd gone out for dinner and drinks with friends in town. We longed for that social freedom and the ability to spend time with close others without the fear of contracting or spreading COVID.

What's the point of that type of nostalgia? Like scholars and scientists of the past, you could imagine that being nostalgic like this is mentally torturous and not especially helpful. It just reminds us of what we can't have in the present. But that isn't how nostalgia works. Instead, these types of nostalgic experiences reminded us that even though we were socially separated during the pandemic, we had family and friends we care about and who care about us. Nostalgia helped us feel mentally connected to others when it was difficult or impossible to have physical interactions with them. Nostalgia operates as a sort of stopgap. As a result, it reduces the negative psychological consequences of feeling lonely or isolated. This is the psychological defense view of nostalgia—we turn to nostalgia to reduce social pain.

Recently a team of researchers led by Xinyue Zhou, a professor of marketing at Zhejiang University in Hangzhou, China, tested nostalgia's potential to combat loneliness during the COVID-19 pandemic, when many people (including me and my wife) were turning to nostalgia because of social isolation.[4] The researchers surveyed people in China, the United States, and the United Kingdom. They found that the lonelier people felt during the pandemic, the less happy they were. No big surprise. But they also found that the lonelier people were, the more they engaged in nostalgia, and that nostalgia helped restore happiness.

> Nostalgia helps us restore our social lives.

In other words, people naturally used nostalgia to combat the pandemic's negative effect on social well-being. If it wasn't for nostalgia, the pandemic might have made countless people even more miserable. There are now quite a few studies documenting nostalgia as a coping resource for loneliness.

It turns out that nostalgia does a lot more than that. Yes, nostalgia counters social pain. It reminds us that we have social connections even when our social lives are suffering. But more than that, nostalgia helps us restore our social lives. By reminding us of fulfilling past social experiences, nostalgia inspires us to prioritize goals that create fulfilling future social experiences.

When my wife and I waxed about past road trips, our nostalgia oriented our minds toward planning trips in the future. When we talked about good times going out with friends, our nostalgia didn't keep us stuck in the past—it encouraged us to plot future parties, dinner outings, and so on. It even motivated us to start planning a major move and job changes so we could live closer to family.

My wife and I aren't alone. During the pandemic, lots of people experienced separation from loved ones and felt inspired to plan future life changes that would allow them to spend more time focused on relationships. For some, this involved looking for a new job or pursuing an entirely different career. For others, this meant planning to relocate to be physically closer to their parents, siblings, or grandchildren. Others decided to retire earlier than planned.

I suspect nostalgia played an important role in guiding many of these decisions. Nostalgia wasn't just the result of social disconnection for these people; it was a resource they used to help determine how they were going to enhance their social lives in the future.

Did you experience social separation during the pandemic? If so, did you find yourself engaging in nostalgia-related activities such as looking at old photos or videos, listening to music from when you were younger, or discussing memories on the phone with family and friends? Did these nostalgic activities help you think about and make plans for the post-pandemic future?

Nostalgia is much more than a defense against negative feelings. Nostalgia puts us on the offense. When we experience nostalgia, we aren't running to the past for protection. We are pulling the past to the present to help us plan the future.

What about nostalgia for experiences that cannot possibly occur in the future? People often have nostalgic memories involving loved ones who are no longer alive. How could that type of nostalgia be future-oriented? Think about it—if you are looking at old photos of a loved one who has passed or you're reminiscing about that person with someone else, you know that you won't be able to see that person again in this lifetime. But that doesn't mean your nostalgia about them is purely past focused. Often our nostalgic longing for people who have died inspires us to better appreciate loved ones who are still alive. We're reminded that life is transient and that the most meaningful experiences are usually the ones we share with family and friends.

We might not be able to connect with those who have passed away, but our nostalgia for them focuses our minds on the importance of relationships. It's easy to get so caught up in day-to-day routines that we neglect to stop and reflect on what we ultimately want out of our lives, what gives us meaning and purpose. Nostalgia helps provide clarity and orients our minds toward the thoughts, feelings, goals, and actions that make life meaningful.

Summary Notes for
"Nostalgia Is about the Future"

- Nostalgia helps us connect with others and steers us toward progress and flourishing.

- People around the world think about and experience nostalgia much the same—as a past-oriented experience often associated with childhood and youth that is typically social in nature.

- Nostalgia being a mixture of positive feelings and a sense of the bittersweet is what distinguishes it from other psychological states and makes it such a complex and powerful experience.

- After spending just minutes engaging in nostalgia, people tend to feel happier, more connected to others, and more grounded in a sense of meaning.

- Nostalgic experiences remind us that even though we might be separated from those we love, we still have family and friends we care about and who care about us.

- By reminding us of treasured social experiences of the past, nostalgia inspires us to act in ways that create such experiences in the future.

CHAPTER 3

WHAT MAKES NOSTALGIA POSSIBLE (AND NECESSARY)

The creative and imaginative energy of children is wonderful to observe because it is raw, innocent, and unconstrained by the responsibilities, worries, and skepticism that come with adulthood. Adults, too, spend a fair amount of time in imaginative thought.

The most popular books, television shows, and movies are often in the fantasy or science-fiction genre. The primary audience for the *Harry Potter* series was obviously children, yet millions of adults (even those without kids at home) enjoyed them. If you've read the *Song of Ice and Fire* books or watched the HBO *Game of Thrones* series, you understand that adults were clearly the target audience, and most parents would agree that the material isn't suitable for children. Despite being aired on premium cable, the *Game of Thrones* finale pulled in nearly twenty million viewers in the US. It's probably impossible to know exactly how many people around the world watched the series, but some estimate that for every one person who paid to watch the show, at least three pirated it. Not to mention the books have sold around one hundred million copies worldwide and have been translated into around fifty languages.

As many movie companies have learned, superheroes aren't just for kids. The ten most successful film franchises of all-time are fantasy-driven. At the top of the list is the Marvel Cinematic Universe that has thus far generated over $22 billion in revenue. Others include franchises such as *Star Wars*, the James Bond movies, *Lord of the Rings*, *The Fast and the Furious*, and *Pirates of the Caribbean*. It's noteworthy that the two franchises that come the closest to realism are about a spy (James Bond) who uses ridiculous gadgets (and has more in common with Batman than any real person doing intelligence work for the government) and a group of race car enthusiasts (the Fast and Furious team) who basically do superhuman stunts using vehicles.

Clearly even full-grown adults enjoy stories and ideas that are beyond the constraints of physical reality. But imagination isn't just a source of entertainment; it's a central feature of what it means to be human. It's also a major factor in why humans have been so successful as a species. We don't just use our imaginations to envision a world full of dragons, wizards, superheroes, aliens, and killer robots; our imaginations inspire the types of scientific and technological advances that previous generations would have considered magical or impossible.

Long before humans ever managed to journey into outer space, they had to imagine it as a possibility. They had to dream. Now that we have accomplished this feat many times, landed on the moon, and sent spacecraft beyond the limits of our solar system, it isn't that hard for us to believe that we will one day establish colonies on other planets. But generations back, this idea would seem like pure science fiction. The world we live in within our minds can ultimately influence the physical world. Imagination is a key ingredient of creation, innovation, and progress. Our imaginations help us generate solutions to current problems, push the human body to new levels of performance, and create works of art that elevate people's spirits.

A good portion of our imaginative energy is dedicated to addressing practical challenges and goals in our daily lives. Say you have applied for a new job and your interview is tomorrow morning. What do you think you are going to be doing tonight when you lie in bed? In all likelihood, unless you are as cool as a cucumber or have no real motivation to do well at the interview, you're going to be running mental simulations in which you imagine what interview questions will be asked and how you'll respond to them. Your mind is plotting. It's preparing for what could occur in the physical world tomorrow. You're making a movie in your mind, writing a script with a successful ending that you hope turns into reality. This is what a professional athlete does to prepare—they visualize a plan and see it unfold in their imagination.

When Alex Honnold became the first person to climb El Capitan in Yosemite National Park with no ropes (free-solo climbing), he had mentally rehearsed the climb countless times and visualized the emotions he would feel at different points. In interviews, Alex noted that in the months leading up to the climb, he removed all social media from his cell phone and stopped responding to emails so that he had more free time to daydream about the details of making the climb. In other words, a good portion of his preparation for this dangerous endeavor took place in his imagination.

Of course, our mental world often implicates the past. If the job interview or athletic competition goes poorly, we often relive it in our mind not just as an act of self-torture but in the service of learning from mistakes and performing better next time. The mental world we live in is rich and dynamic. It's a place where we do a lot of work to learn, grow, and ultimately improve our life in the physical world.

We are better able to control our behavior when we think about how it connects to our self-concepts.

To understand the world within our mind and the psychology of nostalgia, it's important to consider the cognitive capacities that make human mental life distinct. Human cognition is extremely complex, but to appreciate the nature and power of nostalgia, I find it useful to focus on three critical features: self-awareness, temporal consciousness, and symbolic thought.

Self-Awareness

Self-awareness represents our ability to reflect on our own existence. Self-awareness isn't distinctly human, but what makes us unique as a species is that we have the capacity to think deeply about our own lives. This empowers us to exercise self-control and ensures that we're not controlled by our impulses.

When we engage in self-reflection, we're more aware of our self-standards. Classic studies in social psychology show that people are more likely to behave ethically when they have just seen themselves in a mirror or heard their own voice in a recording.[1] It can be jarring to hear our own voice this way. It often feels strange, but it serves to heighten our attention and be more self-critical. Situations that turn our attention toward the self make us more inclined to act in accord with our moral standards. Situations that deindividuate us (such as being part of a mob) or reduce our self-awareness (being drunk, for example) make us less inclined to act in accord with our moral standards.

More broadly, we are better able to control our behavior when we think about how it connects to our self-concepts. Self-concepts are essentially our answer to the question "Who am I?" They're made up of what are called self-schemas—the narratives and identities that we believe define us.

Our high levels of self-awareness orient us toward striving to align our actions with how we define ourselves. For example, we're more likely to take up physical exercise or adopt a healthier diet if we view being healthy as an important part of our self-concept. We often use labels to capture these features of the self-concept—for example, we start to think of ourselves as a "health nut" or "gym rat." We use all sorts of labels to represent and broadcast our self-schemas.

High levels of self-awareness help us coordinate our goals and behaviors in the service of living an intentional life. Obviously we sometimes fall short of our self-standards and engage in behavior that conflicts with our self-concepts. For instance, when angry, we may say something hurtful to those we love—something we wouldn't say otherwise that leaves us feeling embarrassed later. We're not flawless self-regulators, but self-awareness allows us to remain in the driver's seat for most of our lives, even if we aren't always good drivers.

High levels of self-awareness also serve our social lives. We're able to empathize with others because we have what is referred to as *theory of mind*. This is the ability to not only think about our own mental states but also consider those of others. When we see other people experience tragedy, we can put ourselves in their heads and hearts and imagine the pain they're experiencing using theory of mind. This helps us feel for them and better connect with them.

It also allows us to successfully create and navigate a complex social world in which people with diverse personalities, life experiences, goals, and deeply held cultural beliefs are able to coexist and come together to tackle the types of challenges that require coordinated group behavior.

Theory of mind helps us share the mental world we live in. One of the best ways to persuade someone to care about an issue is to use personal stories. You can show people scientific evidence all day long but a more personal appeal is more likely to move them.

Take the issue of homelessness. Showing people statistics of a growing homelessness problem in a major city is useful. It helps people appreciate the size of the problem. But if you illustrate the problem through stories about real people who are homeless and what their daily lives are like, you make them more sympathetic toward the cause.

I have a friend who's a busy attorney. He once spent the night on the street in a cardboard box to better understand the experience of being without adequate shelter. This brief experience of sleeping outside with little protection from the elements helped him gain an understanding of how it feels to be vulnerable in a way he would not normally feel in his everyday life. It inspired him to volunteer his time and donate money to help combat homelessness. His account was made more powerful when he recounted this story to others, including me. When we think about real people and their struggles, our self-awareness helps us access their suffering because we can imagine what it would feel like to be in that situation ourselves.

> Our imaginations manifest in real-world behavior.

Temporal Consciousness

Not only are humans highly self-aware, we're also mental time travelers. In our minds, we can travel to the past and to the future. This also matters for self-control. The previous job-interview example illustrates how self-awareness and temporal consciousness work together. Imagining tomorrow's job interview is an exercise in mental time travel; it involves projecting the self into a possible future. Once the job interview is over, we may be inclined to mentally travel back in time to review our performance, especially if we are seeking self-improvement. As with self-awareness, other animals may have some capacity for temporal consciousness, but humans possess it to a noteworthy degree. We can think about events that happened when we were very young as well as events that occurred way before we were born. We can also imagine a distant future—one that exists long after we're gone.

We can also imagine the lives of others, past and present. The concept of linked lives means we are connected to those closest to us and, by extension, we incorporate their stories alongside ours. For example, a grandparent who lived through a trying time, such as the Great Depression, may pass down behaviors based on the hardships they experienced at that time. This information is passed down from parent or grandparent to child or grandchild. Practices such as keeping plastic butter containers for leftovers and prioritizing time together over material indulgences hearken to tougher times when resources were scarcer and mortality more in question. Our imaginations manifest in real-world behavior and further add to our collective experiences that we may also pass on to the next generation.

Temporal consciousness allows us to be a goal-focused species. Humans will spend a considerable amount of time dedicated to a goal because we are able to imagine a future on the other side of that goal. A few years back, I trained for a half marathon. I was never much of a long-distance runner, so the first few weeks of training were rough. It was hard to imagine that I'd be able to run thirteen miles when five miles proved so grueling, but I knew that if I kept running and adding distance, little by little the future version of myself would be able to do it. I could mentally time travel months ahead and imagine crossing the finish line.

Think about a major goal in your life. Whether it's buying a house, retiring early, traveling around the world, building a successful business, or getting in shape, would you be able to pursue that goal if you weren't able to imagine the future? Goals naturally involve mental time travel because they require efforts to make progress across time.

Being able to imagine the future might seem like a no-brainer, but our goals also involve traveling into the past. Appreciating this will give you some insight into the future-oriented nature of nostalgia.

Think about how the ability to mentally time travel may play a role in pursuing your future-oriented goals. What meaningful or impactful life experiences helped shape your current goals? What past failures and successes (or tragedies and triumphs) helped shape your goals and how you are currently approaching them? What experiences have helped you think about how your goals will benefit you and perhaps those you care about?

Past experiences shape our expectations of how the world works. They also provide vital evidence when we're trying to answer questions about what matters in life. For instance, when choosing a career, you might reflect on the people you thought of as role models growing up as sources of career inspiration. We also look back when thinking about mistakes or problems we would like to avoid, connecting those memories to present choices and considering how they might influence our futures. We understand that the decisions we make today impact our lives tomorrow.

Symbolic Thought

A critical feature of our imaginative mental life is our ability to think symbolically. You're able to understand the words in this book because your brain possesses the capacity to understand symbols. When you see the word *pizza*, you can conjure in your mind a segmented circle of baked dough accompanied with sauce, cheese, and other toppings.

Thanks to your capacity for symbolic thought, what might otherwise be a series of strange and meaningless lines translates to words that ultimately represent ideas. I don't have to show an actual pizza to communicate the concept of a pizza to you.

Societies were built on the ability to think symbolically. Symbols don't just operate as abstractions of concrete things for the sake of communication. They also stir our emotions by representing fundamental beliefs, important identities, and meaningful life experiences.

Here's a notable example: In the United States, about 50 percent of people think it should be illegal to burn the American flag, and even more find the act offensive (even if they respect people's freedom to do it).[2] Why do so many Americans feel this way? The vast majority report that they are proud of their national identity. For them, the flag is more than a piece of cloth; it symbolizes their core beliefs and identity.

Social psychologists have conducted problem-solving studies showing that people are extremely reluctant to use cherished cultural symbols in ways that feel inappropriate. For example, research participants in one study were asked to nail an object to the wall and were told to use any other object in the room that would help them complete the task. The problem, they soon discovered, was that the only item available that would function as a hammer was a crucifix. The researchers observed that participants went to great lengths to avoid treating the crucifix as a hammer; when they ultimately did, it made them feel uncomfortable. Another study found similar effects when research participants needed to damage an American flag to solve a problem they were working on.[3]

Our capacity for complex symbolic thought can also be observed in our frequent use of metaphors. There is now a large body of research on the extent to which humans use metaphor to think about and communicate ideas. Scholars have analyzed large volumes of different types of texts such as academic books, news reporting, fiction stories, and transcribed conversations and have found that between 8 and 19 percent of English language discourse is metaphorical in nature.[4]

People tend to think of metaphor as purely a linguistic tool—a way to make stories, poems, and other forms of written communication more colorful or artistic. But cognitive scientists have discovered that metaphors are much more than that.

Metaphors help us understand and communicate abstract ideas by mapping them onto more concrete concepts. For instance, when someone is described as "a ray of sunshine," everyone understands that the person being described isn't actually a beam emanating from the sun. People understand that a metaphoric description is being employed to illustrate positive characteristics (using yet another metaphor, this person "brightens" your day), because we associate sunshine and brightness with warmth and other positive states.

A few years ago, my colleagues and I conducted some research on how metaphors related to the self-concept connected to religious faith and spirituality.[5] In our studies, we asked research participants the following question: "Regardless of what you know about biology, which body part do you more closely associate with your self?" They were given two options to choose from: brain or heart. Consistent with previous research, we found that the participants were almost equally divided. About half chose heart and half chose brain.

Since at least the time of Plato, Westerners have used head and heart metaphors to represent different styles of thinking. To use one's head is associated with thinking logically or rationally. To use one's heart is associated with relying on intuition and emotion. When people are advised to trust their intuitions or feelings, they're told to follow their hearts. When they're advised to think critically, they're told to use their heads.

In our studies, we were interested if we could use this simple self-location metaphor task to predict people's belief in God and level of religiosity. A large body of research shows that religious and spiritual beliefs are related more to intuitive thinking than rational thinking. Some people are critical of intuition, but it turns out that it plays an important role in life experiences that give us meaning. Feelings like awe, wonder, love, hope, and inspiration rely on intuition. When people engage in difficult problem-solving tasks that involve math, science, or logic, they benefit from rational thinking. But when they seek spiritual connection, intuitive cognitive processes are needed.

Based on this, we reasoned that people who generally think of themselves as heart people would identify as more religious than those who generally think of themselves as head people. And this is exactly what we found. In reality, people are a mix of head and heart, rationality and intuition. A scientist or attorney can use rational thinking skills to do their jobs and switch to intuition to fully experience social and spiritual life.

A Complex Cognitive Cocktail

Together, our high levels of self-awareness, temporal consciousness, and symbolic thought provide us a rich and dynamic mental world to inhabit. Science-fiction movies and books imagine a future in which people spend much of their time in a virtual world. Perhaps one day even physical death will be defeated by technological innovations that allow for a person's consciousness to be removed from the body and uploaded to the cloud (another metaphorical framing). Whether or not these science-fiction ideas become reality, the fact that we can imagine them as possible says a lot about our species. Our brains use a considerable amount of our energy, about 20 percent of what our total body uses—more than any other organ.[6] The mental world we live in is a major part of our lives. It involves our hopes and fears, memories and aspirations, efforts to understand what others think and feel, and all sorts of other activities that make being human so interesting.

The complete story of what makes our mental life so unique is far more complicated than what I just described, as it involves a number of brain mechanisms and processes, but this brief overview sets the stage for a deeper understanding of how nostalgia is possible and necessary.

The Mental World of Nostalgia

Nostalgia is a complex cognitive and emotional experience. It requires the three cognitive capacities just discussed: high levels of self-awareness, temporal consciousness, and symbolic thought. When we experience nostalgia, we use our ability to mentally time travel to revisit the past, but it's more complicated than that.

Nostalgia is typically self-focused. I don't mean that nostalgia is necessarily selfish. In fact, nostalgia makes people kinder and more helpful to others. By self-focused I simply mean that much of the time our nostalgic feelings involve experiences from our own past.

Individuals can also be nostalgic about nonautobiographical aspects of the past. Indeed, all sorts of artistic and entertainment-driven hobbies and interests involve nostalgia for a time long ago. For instance, an antique collector may have nostalgic feelings for a period in history long before they were born (this falls into the category of what is referred to as *historical nostalgia*). But most of the time, when humans feel the pull of nostalgia, it's about some part of their own lives. Nostalgia typically focuses on the self-story.

Nostalgia plays a key role in helping people manage vulnerabilities.

Finally, nostalgia uses symbolic thought. Think about all the memorabilia people keep as symbolic representations of cherished memories or family heirlooms that are passed down from generation to generation that symbolize intergenerational nostalgia, weaving together individual self-stories across time to craft a broader family story via their linked lives.

Nostalgia as a Necessity

Nostalgia relies on complex cognitive capacities that appear to be uniquely human, but this doesn't explain why people experience nostalgia—and often quite frequently. My colleagues and I have found that around 80 percent of people report feeling nostalgic at least once a week, and nearly half report feeling nostalgic several times a week.[7]

The bulk of this book is dedicated to describing the many functions nostalgia serves and how we can best take advantage of those functions. But it's first important to understand that nostalgia is a necessity. The same cognitive capacities that have helped humans flourish as self-disciplined, creative, innovative, and goal-driven organisms have also generated unique vulnerabilities. Nostalgia plays a key role in helping people manage these vulnerabilities.

For example, public speaking is a common fear among people. It typically isn't physically dangerous to stand in front of a group and share your ideas or experiences, but the high levels of self-awareness that help us in so many ways also make us incredibly self-conscious. We worry that people will ridicule us. We ruminate and doubt our competence. We fear that we will stumble. Because we can mentally time travel to the future, we can imagine all sorts of negative consequences for a poor performance: *If I screw up my presentation at the big meeting, will I hurt my chance for future promotions? Will my reputation in the office be harmed for years to come?*

As we become increasingly self-conscious as we grow up, we start worrying about what others think about us. This concern comes with some benefits, because receiving social feedback can help us develop social skills that help us get along well with others. But the more we worry about what others think, the more likely we are to become anxious and sad when others are inconsiderate or cruel.

In short, with great intelligence comes great anxiety. It turns out that nostalgia is a psychological resource we naturally use to counter the uncertainties and anxieties that are part of being a highly intelligent organism. Nostalgia helps us make sense of our lives and gives us direction. This book will help you develop strategies for getting the most out of nostalgia, but even people who have never read a single sentence about the scientific research on the benefits of nostalgia naturally use it to find comfort and motivation, even if they don't realize they're doing so.

When people experience life events that are painful, chaotic, and anxiety-provoking, they often look to the past to restore well-being and find hope. Learning how nostalgia works, the different ways it serves human flourishing, and specific strategies to get the most out of nostalgia can help you live a richer and fuller life.

Summary Notes for "What Makes Nostalgia Possible (and Necessary)"

- Imagination helps us solve problems, create and pursue goals, connect with others, make art, and much more.

- There are three cognitive capacities pertaining to nostalgia that make human mental life distinct: self-awareness, temporal consciousness, and symbolic thought.

- Self-awareness allows us to reflect on our existence and empowers us to exercise self-control.

- Temporal consciousness means that our minds can travel to the past and the future. Goals involve mental time travel because they require us to sustain effort across time.

- Symbols allow us to communicate, represent our beliefs and identities, and describe meaningful life experiences.

- Nostalgia is a psychological resource that helps us counter the uncertainties and anxieties that come with being a highly intelligent organism.

PART 2

HOW NOSTALGIA ENHANCES THE SELF

CHAPTER 4

NOSTALGIA SHAPES
THE SELF-CONCEPT

Who am I? What are the cultural and social identities, roles, life experiences, personality traits, and other attributes that make me the person I am today? Am I the same person I used to be, or have I changed in fundamental ways? Do I truly know myself, or is it possible that I'm living a lie, disconnected from who I am deep down? Can other people really know me?

You might not ask yourself such questions so directly or in this exact way, but most humans grapple with these issues at some point in their lives. Because we're the most highly self-aware organisms on the planet, we spend a considerable amount of time in our own heads exploring, crafting, maintaining, and protecting our sense of self.

Psychologists have long studied the idea of the self. As a result, there is an extremely large and diverse body of research concerning different aspects of the self and how they influence our feelings, beliefs, goals, and behaviors.

What exactly is the self? The American Psychological Association (APA) defines the self as "the totality of the individual, consisting of all characteristic attributes, conscious and unconscious, mental and physical."[1] This is a broad definition, probably because the self is a broad construct. Accordingly, when research psychologists study the self, they focus on specific self-features and processes (such as personality or motivation).

One central feature of the self is the *self-concept*. Essentially, the self-concept is how we answer the question "Who am I?" It's our identity—or, more precisely, our identities, because all of us have many of them. The very same person could identify as a mother in one context and a wife, accountant, runner, reader, gardener, or antique collector in another. Such categories only paint part of the picture of the self because each identity involves varying levels of what psychologists call *self-centrality*, which is how important a given identity is to one's overall self-concept.

The more central an identity is to our self-concept, the more motivated we are by that identity. We're also more sensitive to perceived successes and failures related to that identity. For example, if being a mother is more central to one's self-concept than being a gardener, that individual will be more likely to prioritize goals and activities related to motherhood over those related to gardening. She will also be more likely to experience positive emotions when feeling like she is doing a good job as a mother as well as negative emotions when assessing otherwise. The self-concept helps us figure out our priorities and ambitions. It also plays a central role in determining what threatens and bolsters our self-esteem.

The self-concept is partially outside of our control because some characteristics that influence how we approach life are at least partly determined by genes and other factors. People don't decide to be introverted or extroverted, for instance, just as people don't decide who their parents are, where they are born, when they are born, and so on. Many of the personality characteristics and life experiences that influence the self-concept occur without our say or intentions.

Nostalgia is a social-oriented experience.

Thanks to our advanced cognitive capacities, however, we decide what defines who we are. We're always faced with the traits and experiences we can't control, but we also have much influence over how to use our assets and approach our challenges. Just as an expert chef can make an outstanding meal by combining all sorts of ingredients, we can shape our self-concept by optimizing the mix of personality traits and experiences we've been dealt.

Nostalgia can play a major role here. Nostalgia helps us craft a life story or narrative we can use to figure out how we want to define the self-concept. We don't determine all the life events that go into our story, but like a director of a film, we're allowed to edit the raw footage to represent who we are and create the story that defines us.

The Protagonists

Given that so many previous scholars, mental health practitioners, and writers have viewed nostalgia as either a disease or psychological vulnerability, my colleagues and I reasoned it was important to get a thorough picture of the content of nostalgic memories. When people reflect on the past, what exactly do they think about?

To answer that question, we examined people's written accounts of nostalgic memories. Fortunately for us, we found *Nostalgia*, a periodical that invited readers to submit nostalgic stories from their personal past. The length of these stories varied from one thousand to fifteen hundred words, and the authors ranged in age from their early twenties to their late eighties. We trained research assistants to code the content of these nostalgic stories, which gave us a starting point for taking a snapshot of what nostalgic memories actually look like.[2]

The most common theme people wrote about was close relationships (family, romantic partners, and friends), followed by momentous life events that typically involved close relationships (weddings, graduations, holidays, and family gatherings). These results suggest that nostalgia is a social-oriented experience—an important point I'll revisit in part 3 of this book.

We also discovered that the self was prominently featured in these stories and typically assumed the role of protagonist. In other words, nostalgic memories are social stories but stories that situate the memory holder's contribution to the experience in the center of the tale. This makes sense, because nostalgic memories are typically revisited from our distinct point of view.

In a second study, to make sure these findings were not specific to the type of people who are inclined to submit personal essays to a magazine about nostalgia, we recruited university students and asked them to write about a nostalgic experience from their lives.[3] The results were quite similar. The most common theme of these stories was close relationships and momentous life events. Again, the self played a central role. Since these studies (conducted nearly twenty years ago), there have been dozens more like them. All of them confirm our original findings.

Nostalgia is autobiographical in nature. When we reflect on the past experiences that make us feel nostalgic, we aren't passive participants in other people's stories. We're also not merely observing the world go by. Nostalgia helps us clarify and define the important roles we play in our social worlds.

Like a movie or play, social life entails various characters playing different roles. Our nostalgic memories highlight our role. They direct our attention to our individual contributions to the broader social and cultural narrative. By doing so, these memories help us figure out who we are.

Bring to mind a memory that makes you feel nostalgic. Immerse yourself in the memory for a while, then spend a few minutes writing about the experience and how it made you feel. After writing, consider what this particular memory reveals about your self-concept. Try engaging in this nostalgic exercise multiple times at regular intervals—maybe once a day or once per week. Each time you do so, bring to mind and write about a different nostalgic memory. Use these different memories to reflect on common themes around your self-concept and the identities that compose your self-concept.

Nostalgia Helps Reveal the True Self

People regularly fail to see how behaviors related to one of their identities affect (and even harm) aspects of their lives that are more central to their self-concept. This occurs because we often operate on autopilot and neglect to examine how our day-to-day behaviors align with what we care about most. It would take forever to get anything done if we carefully analyzed each of our actions, so it's useful to automate our behavior. Much of the time we just need to move forward and get stuff done, not overthink every decision.

But the downside is allowing our behaviors to be shaped by social and cultural trends as opposed to the identities and related goals we find to be more central to how we define ourselves. For instance, we might strongly believe that being a good parent is more important to our self-concept than accumulating and displaying material wealth, but then we find ourselves working all the time and never seeing our family in order to live in an expensive neighborhood and drive a fancy car. We might not have consciously decided to put material gain and status over family, but such things can happen if we're not mindful. Aligning with our self-concept requires conscious decision-making.

> Nostalgic memories are often self-defining; they help us write and understand our self-story.

Nostalgia can help us refocus our attention on what's most important. Nostalgic memories are often self-defining; they help us write and understand our self-story. As already noted, studies show that the self is the protagonist in nostalgic memories. In addition, studies show that people feel like nostalgic memories capture what is central to their self-concept more than other types of autobiographical memories.

For example, in one experiment exploring how different types of memories influence how people feel about themselves, a research team led by Elena Stephan, a professor of psychology at Bar-Ilan University in Israel, randomly assigned British participants to write about a nostalgic memory, a positive memory, or an ordinary memory.[4] The researchers wanted to see if the memories people identify as nostalgic affect their sense of self differently than other memories—namely, those they view as happy but not necessarily nostalgic and memories that are more mundane.

After writing about one of these memories, research participants were asked to report the extent to which the memory they just described reflects on them as a person. The researchers found that people who wrote about a nostalgic memory were significantly more likely to view that memory as reflecting who they truly are than those who wrote about a positive or ordinary memory. This study supports the idea that nostalgic memories tap into what is central to the self-concept more than non-nostalgic memories.

Another study explored this idea in a different way. A research team led by Alison Lenton at the University of Southampton in the UK asked individuals to write about an experience that made them feel most like their real self or an experience that made them feel less so.[5] After writing about one of these experiences, they were asked to indicate how much they felt nostalgic for the past experience they just described. People who wrote about an experience that made them feel more like their real self were more nostalgic for the experience than those who wrote about an experience that made them feel less like their real self.

Other research conducted by Matthew Baldwin and a team at the University of Kansas expanded on these findings to explore nostalgia's potential to help people focus on aligning their lives with what they found central to their self-concept.[6] In their first study, the researchers asked people to bring to mind one memory from their past and to think about it for a few minutes. The study participants then responded to questions concerning how much thinking about that memory made them feel nostalgic. Next, they were asked to report how much they currently felt aware of who they truly are and to what extent they were focused on social approval.

The researchers found that when people reflect on past memories, the more those memories make them feel nostalgic, the more they feel aware of who they truly are and the less they feel concerned with what others think about them. In other words, this study reveals that nostalgia orients people toward the experiences and goals that are most important to their self-concept and away from the endeavors that are more about social approval.

These researchers conducted other studies to further test nostalgia as a tool people use to live a more intentional life focused on what they find most central to their self-concepts.[7] For example, they conducted experiments that showed that after people spend a few minutes writing about a nostalgic memory (compared to a non-nostalgic memory), they feel more like they understand their true self. They also found that people who more frequently engage in nostalgia are more likely to feel like they understand their true self than people who aren't nostalgic as frequently.

Here's a telling example of the self-clarifying nature of nostalgia from one of the studies my colleagues and I conducted: A research participant shared a memory focused on how he started to develop a love for farming. He described riding in the combine with his dad after school, and he remembered being excited every day to be able to do that. He further indicated that these experiences were the best times of his childhood.

Memories of all types are useful in different ways. We use our experiences via memories to help us avoid future pitfalls or to inform current decisions when the path forward is uncertain. Both past successes and failures offer guidance on how to make decisions in the present and how we might better plan for the future. And studies reveal that nostalgic memories are particularly useful for helping us understand our self-concepts and focus our energy on the aspects of the self-concept we care about most and want to truly define us.

Bring to mind a nostalgic memory involving a life experience that you believe truly captures a central feature of your self-concept. Spend a few minutes writing about this experience and the aspect of your self-concept it reveals. Now, reflect on your current life. Do you think the way you're living today supports this central feature? If not, is this something you would like to change? If so, try to come up with at least one specific goal that would help you move toward supporting that part of your self-concept. Use the nostalgic memory you reflected on (and others) to help you identify activities that would allow you to reconnect with that central feature of your self-concept.

For example, in your nostalgic memory, what were you doing that allowed this important aspect of your self-concept to be expressed? Are there similar activities that you could do today?

As we age and our life circumstances and responsibilities change, we may feel like we can no longer do certain things we consider to be self-defining, and that can make us feel like we're losing central features of our self-concept. Often the main limitation is our imagination. For example, maybe in your young adult years you were a competitive long-distance runner. Now that you're older and busy with your career and kids, perhaps you don't have the time to train as you once did. Or maybe the wear and tear on your body is a barrier. You look back nostalgically on when you were at your competitive peak and realize that that time of your life is over. How can nostalgia possibly support you reasserting that athletic identity?

You can't repeat the past. But remember: that's not the function of nostalgia. Nostalgia won't revitalize your youthful body, but it can help you revitalize your youthful spirit, the mental characteristics that created that central identity to begin with.

What can you do today to push yourself the way you had to mentally and physically push yourself when you were younger? There are all sorts of ways to test your self-discipline and focus. Maybe this means a new type of physical activity, but it doesn't have to. What matters is the mindset—that feeling of agency, self-expression, accomplishment, and growth. Nostalgia can help reignite that.

Self-Continuity

Figuring out and regularly reminding ourselves of what we find most important to our self-concept is an important part of living an intentional and authentic life. But the self exists across time. We don't just live in the present. If we did, there would be no nostalgia. Since humans are cognitively advanced and able to mentally time travel, we also care about how we define the self across time. We think about who we used to be and how that helps us understand who we are in the present. We also connect the past self and the present self with an imagined future self.

To appreciate this, think about an important self-improvement goal. Maybe you want to eat a healthier diet. To do so, you might imagine a future self-concept that is more health focused. To accomplish this, you look at what you are doing today to make appropriate changes, but you also look at your past self. Maybe you once ate healthier but life became busy and you started eating more junk food. Or maybe you always had an unhealthy diet but other lessons from your past can help you imagine a healthier self. For instance, maybe your past experience pursuing a career goal can give you some insight into how to create the type of structure that could help you succeed with a healthy eating goal.

> The more people view their past self and present self as connected, the more mentally and physically healthy they tend to be.

Connecting different self-defining life experiences across time helps us in various ways. We are highly motivated to make connections across time that help us maintain what scholars refer to as *self-continuity*. This is the feeling that we have a stable self across time, that the person we were years ago is connected to the person we are now and the person we will be in the future.

Most people recognize and appreciate that they've changed over time. I suspect most people are happy that they have different attitudes and perspectives than when they were much younger and had less life experience. Personal growth is usually desirable; even so, we still have a strong need for self-stability.

To appreciate this, consider the extreme example of a total loss of self. Some accidents and neurological diseases have the capacity to rob us of our memories and dramatically change our personalities. Our bodies age and change, but we want to feel like the self remains largely intact over time. And for good reason. Psychologists have documented the importance of self-continuity for human flourishing—the more people view their past self and present self as connected, the more mentally and physically healthy they tend to be. In addition, *self-discontinuity*—the sense that one's past self and present self are disjointed—is associated with psychological distress and suicide.[8]

The idea that nostalgia may serve our need for self-continuity dates back a couple of decades. As mentioned in chapter 1, the sociologist Fred Davis suggested in 1979 that nostalgia may help maintain or restore self-continuity when people face life experiences that make them feel disconnected from their pasts by "encouraging an appreciative stance toward former selves; excluding unpleasant memories; reinterpreting 'marginal, fugitive, and eccentric facets of earlier selves' in a positive light; and establishing benchmarks of one's biography."[9]

Building on Davis's theorizing, a number of studies show how nostalgia helps people cope with experiences that cause self-discontinuity as well as increase feelings of self-continuity. In one such study, my colleagues and I wanted to see if people naturally become more nostalgic when dealing with life experiences that have the potential to cause feelings of self-discontinuity.[10] To test this, we gave research participants a list of life events that are typically associated with self-discontinuity: divorce, the death of a spouse, and changes in residence, financial status, sleeping habits, and so on. We asked participants to indicate whether they had experienced each of these events and then respond to questions regarding how frequently they felt nostalgic. We then tallied the number of life changes each reported to see if people who have experienced more changes are more frequently nostalgic. We found that they are.

Of course, just because we found that more life changes are associated with more nostalgia doesn't directly provide evidence that people turn to nostalgia in response to life experiences that cause self-discontinuity or that nostalgia actually helps people maintain self-continuity. In addition, given that people value positive changes that are associated with personal growth, my colleagues and I thought that people would only turn to nostalgia as a way to restore self-continuity when the changes they experience are negative. Said differently, we reasoned that people need nostalgia most when discontinuity threatens the connections to the past they truly value.

To test these ideas more explicitly, we conducted additional studies.[11] In one, we took advantage of the fact that university students are naturally experiencing a time of substantial change. Many have moved away from family and friends and are grappling with major decisions (and anxieties) about their futures. All of this can make students feel unstable and disconnected from their old self and the relationships that have thus far helped define who they are. At the same time, the university years are often a time of personal growth, as students are exposed to new ideas and meet people from different parts of the country and even different parts of the world. These fresh experiences can help students clarify who they are and encourage them to pursue goals that align with their self-concept.

We recruited a large sample of undergraduates and divided them into three groups. All of them were informed that they were going to read an essay based on psychological research that described the consequences of transitioning to study at a university. In actuality, each group read distinct essays: one group was provided an essay that encouraged them to think about the university years as a time of negative change, another group read an essay that spoke of college as a time of positive change and personal growth, and yet a third group read an essay that advocated the university years as a time of stability. After reading their assigned essay, participants completed a questionnaire asking them how nostalgic they were for different aspects of their past. Using these three different essays allowed us to determine if any type of discontinuity increases nostalgia or if it is particularly negative discontinuity that makes people look to the past nostalgically.

We found that nostalgia is a response to negative discontinuity. Research participants who read either the essay indicating that the university years are a time of positive change or the essay indicating that the university years are a time of stability reported similar levels of nostalgia. However, those participants who were informed that college was associated with negative change reported significantly higher levels of nostalgia than the other two groups. People are more likely to feel nostalgic when they feel like the life changes they are experiencing are negative.

This finding and others indicate that people don't tend to turn to nostalgia anytime there is change in their lives but specifically when they are navigating the types of changes that can make them feel as if they are losing the social connections, values, and beliefs about themselves that support a stable self-concept across time.

But just because people become nostalgic as a response to negative self-discontinuity doesn't prove that nostalgia actually helps people maintain self-continuity. Looking into this issue further, we recruited another sample of university students and divided them into three groups.[12] One was asked to spend a few minutes thinking about an experience that made them feel nostalgic, another was prompted to bring to mind an ordinary experience from their past, and a third group was asked to contemplate a positive event from their life (we included this latter group to determine if nostalgia helps people maintain self-continuity more than positive thinking). All participants then completed a questionnaire that measured feelings of self-continuity. It included items such as "I feel connected with who I was in the past" and "There is continuity in my life."

We found that participants who reflected on a nostalgic experience endorsed these sentences more than those who reflected on an ordinary experience or positive life event. This suggests that nostalgia uniquely helps people feel connected to their past. Other studies my colleagues and I conducted also found that the self-continuity that nostalgia helps provide increases psychological well-being.[13]

Recent studies conducted by Sanda Ismail, a professor of public health at the University of the West of England, and his colleagues have shown that nostalgia serves a similar self-continuity function for people who are especially vulnerable to discontinuity—individuals living with dementia.[14] Ismail's team found that nostalgic memories among these people are similar in content to the nostalgic memories of people who do not suffer from dementia. Despite their cognitive impairment, individuals living with dementia experience nostalgia similarly to cognitively healthy individuals. The researchers also found that among individuals with mild to moderate levels of dementia, nostalgia increases feelings of self-continuity.

Researchers are now working to develop workbooks and other interventions that can potentially help people living with dementia, and their families and caregivers benefit from nostalgia while navigating the personal and social challenges caused by cognitive decline. Autobiographical memory loss and other cognitive challenges caused by dementia can lead to an impaired and fragmented sense of self. Nostalgia can't prevent the inevitable decline, but it may help people maintain their sense of self for longer, improving their quality of life.

When you experience major changes in your life that you find unpleasant, take some time to reflect on nostalgic memories and explore how they might help you maintain a stable sense of self across time.

Nostalgic memories travel with us through the sometimes uncertain and unpleasant journey of life. I was recently watching a news story about people in California who lost their homes to wildfires. They were obviously upset, but nearly all of them expressed gratitude for having escaped with their lives. Most noted that they could replace their possessions but not the people who were important to them. An interview with one older man stood out to me: he said that the fire had taken his house but it couldn't erase the memories that he and his family made in that house.

The Future Self

So far I've described how nostalgia helps people understand and prioritize what's most important to their self-concepts and preserve a stable self-concept across time. The research covered in this chapter also helps reveal something about nostalgia that points to the guiding theme of this book: nostalgia involves past experiences, but it's really about helping people move forward in life.

We want to make decisions that lead to personal fulfillment and flourishing. It can be distressing when we feel like our pursuits don't serve our true self, and we regularly lose our passion for activities that begin to feel disconnected from who we truly are. In fact, quite a few studies indicate that people are most satisfied pursuing goals (and are most likely to complete them) when they view that goal as internally motivated by the self-concept and not externally motivated by things like money, social status, and social approval.

If you ever feel lost or like you've become disconnected from your true self and aren't sure what direction to take in life, the best path forward might be revealed by looking to the past.

Think about the different life experiences that make you feel nostalgic. What do they tell you about the part of you that is most central to your self-concept, the part of you that you want to reconnect with and build upon to live a more intentional life?

Summary Notes for "Nostalgia Shapes the Self-Concept"

- The self-concept is our identity or set of identities. The more central an identity is to our self-concept, the more motivated we are by it.

- The self-concept is not totally under our control because genetics and other factors play significant roles. However, all of us are still able to influence our self-concept to a large degree.

- We are more likely to pursue and complete goals that are internally motivated by the self-concept. Nostalgia steers us toward experiences and goals that are more in line with our self-concept and away from activities that have more to do with social approval.

- Self-continuity is the sense of a stable self across time. Nostalgia helps us deal with experiences that cause self-discontinuity; it also increases our feelings of self-continuity.

- We tend to feel nostalgic when experiencing negative changes in our lives.

CHAPTER 5

NOSTALGIA BUILDS HEALTHY SELF-ESTEEM

One of the main challenges of being a highly self-conscious but also extremely social organism is that we are often worried about what others think of us, and this tendency is connected to how we think about ourselves. In the modern world—especially in the highly individualistic modern Western world—we are encouraged to love ourselves no matter what others think, to celebrate our uniqueness, and to publicly express ourselves with confidence. Even so, it's hard to escape the natural inclination to base our self-esteem on the approval of others.

That said, undeserved self-confidence can cause personal and professional problems. Narcissists, for instance, have an inflated view of themselves that's often immune to feedback and critique (which makes them notably difficult to work with and nearly impossible to live with). When other people offer narcissists useful feedback, they tend to become defensive, even aggressive.

On the other hand, self-loathing can lead to a host of personal and professional problems. People suffering from depression often have a low sense of self-worth even when other people value them. Therapy to treat depression often focuses on such cognitive distortions. The therapist works to help the client understand that they have a negatively biased view of reality, with the end goal being to help the client develop cognitive tools they can use to disrupt their distorted thinking and take on a more positive way of thinking.

All of this indicates that, at some level, it's good for our self-evaluations to connect with our social worlds and, within reason, to be influenced by what other people think of us. Society wouldn't function well if everyone's self-views were disconnected from social feedback and judgment. Of course, this doesn't always go well. Children are often teased and bullied, leading to low self-esteem and sadness. But this doesn't mean it's wrong to be sensitive to social approval. It means it's wrong for people to be socially cruel.

However, we can't control how other people treat us, and we don't always have a say regarding the social circles we inhabit. As we age, we may gain more power over where we live and work and who we spend our time with, but life will always involve navigating a social world with people of all sorts—those who positively contribute to our lives as well as those who cause us pain and suffering.

When it comes to our self-esteem, it's best to balance seeking social approval with developing psychological resources that help us maintain or restore self-esteem when others behave unfairly or cruelly. It's also important that we learn to respond productively and nondefensively when we experience situations that harm our self-esteem because of our own failures and shortcomings. Nostalgia is a psychological resource that serves these functions. It can help us achieve and preserve resilient, growth-oriented self-esteem.

Why Care about Self-Esteem?

There are some who believe that focusing on self-esteem is a problem, that we should instead pay more attention to psychological characteristics like self-control. They have a point, especially when you consider how self-esteem became popularized in the United States in ways that potentially contributed to a rise in narcissism and social disconnection.

We've all heard stories of over-affirming acts (such as handing out participation trophies to anyone who participates) and overindulgent parenting that might unintentionally encourage kids to develop a sense of entitlement and a lack of humility and empathy. We've also seen how consumerism, insecurity, and vanity combine to generate an array of social, psychological, and financial problems. People regularly go into serious debt from buying cars, houses, jewelry, clothing, and other products that portray a certain public image.

The self-esteem movement championed by some psychologists and educators over the last few decades has failed to produce the type of academic outcomes that were predicted. Efforts to boost self-esteem in schools, for instance, didn't result in kids being better students. And rates of depression and anxiety have been increasing among young people in recent decades, at the same time there's been more emphasis placed on affirming kids' self-esteem.[1] Self-esteem clearly isn't everything. It's even possible that some of the strategies we've employed to promote self-esteem have contributed to certain social ills and psychological vulnerabilities.

Some scholars have even argued that self-esteem is a uniquely Western endeavor, that people in non-Western countries aren't concerned about feeling good about themselves, but this view isn't well supported by research. Self-esteem seems to be a universal need, even if people in different cultures pursue it in distinct ways.[2] It seems clear that humans all over the world are interested in enjoying a positive view of self. They want to believe they're living up to the social and cultural standards they personally identify with.

People need healthy levels of self-esteem to adaptively function.

Even if you think we value the wrong sources of self-esteem in our society or that we put too much emphasis on self-esteem at the expense of other psychological traits, the fact remains that self-esteem is important to overall well-being. Low self-esteem is associated with a wide range of psychological and physical health problems, and high self-esteem can make people overconfident, narcissistic, and hostile. But low self-esteem is demotivating and depressing; it makes people less likely to want to take care of themselves and help others. People need healthy levels of self-esteem to adaptively function, and here's another place that nostalgia can help.

Nostalgia Supports Healthy Self-Esteem

When my colleagues and I first started to conduct research on the psychology of nostalgia, we wanted to test the basic hypothesis that nostalgia would increase self-esteem. We had a number of reasons to suspect that it would. First, as discussed in the previous chapter, nostalgia involves the self in the role of protagonist. Our nostalgic memories help us see the important roles we play in the world, which should affirm a positive view of self. Second, nostalgic memories are social; they feature the people we care most about. Self-esteem is social, too. It tends to increase when we feel loved and valued, and it usually decreases when we feel rejected and undervalued. Our analyses of the content of nostalgic memories revealed that they are more likely to involve feeling loved and valued, which should affirm a positive view of self. Third, nostalgic memories are cherished memories. They remind us that even though life can be difficult and uncertain, even unbearably painful at times, it's also full of rewarding experiences, and that should also affirm a positive view of self.

In one of our experiments, we had some research participants write about a nostalgic experience and others write about a non-nostalgic life experience. After this, participants in both groups completed a questionnaire that asked them to rate their level of agreement with statements such as "I take a positive attitude toward myself" and "On the whole, I am satisfied with myself." Not surprisingly, we found that participants who wrote about a nostalgic experiences reported significantly higher self-esteem than those who didn't.[3] Since conducting this experiment almost twenty years ago, many other studies have also found that when people experience nostalgia, they tend to receive a boost in self-esteem.[4]

Lots of activities and experiences can increase self-esteem, but not all sources of self-esteem are the same. For example, some people derive self-esteem from physical beauty, but physical attractiveness tends to be associated with youth, and youth doesn't last long. Americans spend billions of dollars on cosmetic surgeries every year. People who undergo procedures such as breast augmentation report that they did so to feel better about themselves, see themselves as they were when they were younger, and other motives that reveal a self-concept and ultimately self-esteem that is connected to their attitudes about physical beauty.

But investing too heavily in physical beauty as a source of self-esteem is ultimately a losing investment; regardless of how many times one goes under the knife or engages in healthy activities such as physical exercise, physical beauty fades with time. An overemphasis on something like beauty can distract one from pursuing richer and longer-lasting sources of self-esteem. In fact, when people reach old age, it's common for them to report wishing they would have spent less time worried about living up to societal standards of status (things like beauty and wealth) and more time focused on their family, friends, and community.

Some efforts to conform to social standards of self-esteem can prove physically harmful. In the early 2000s, tanning salons were popular, particularly among female college students. Some researchers had found that the more teen girls and young women reported that being physically attractive was important to their self-esteem, the more motivated they were to tan, even though doing so put them at increased risk for skin cancer. In a study I worked on, we found that when such young women were focused on increasing their self-esteem, they became more motivated to tan, especially if they were exposed to media that associated tan skin with beauty, such as advertisements that featured sexually attractive women in bikinis with tanned skin.[5]

The good news was that we were also able to reduce interest in tanning in our studies. Interestingly, it wasn't because we convinced young women to be concerned about the physical dangers of tanning; instead, we were able to reduce tanning because we presented them with media materials that made them more likely to find pale skin to be beautiful. We showed them articles and photos of popular celebrities from that era (like Gwyneth Paltrow) who were perceived as beautiful but didn't possess tanned skin.

Other researchers have found that young men drive faster and more recklessly in the pursuit of self-esteem because they associate risk-taking behavior with being tough and cool.[6] This reveals something that social psychologists have learned about the power of self-esteem. People prioritize self-esteem over physical health in large part because the threat to health is often abstract, whereas the threat to self-esteem is more immediate and feels certain. Also, the need for social approval is strong, especially in young people. It may seem silly, but being sensitive to what others think has helped our species survive and thrive. Even so, it's crucial that people develop sources of self-esteem that are connected to the social world but also healthy and sustainable. Nostalgia can help cultivate and maintain this type of self-esteem.

Nostalgic memories are connected to the social world because they typically involve social experiences. But here's the important part: nostalgia orients people toward intrinsic social relationships, not extrinsic ones. Intrinsic social relationships are the connections we have with people who value us for our internal characteristics—who we truly are. These tend to be deep and enduring relationships. Extrinsic social relationships, on the other hand, involve people who value us for external characteristics such as beauty, status, wealth, and so on. These are more superficial relationships that tend to be fragile and transient. The more people focus on cultivating and maintaining intrinsic social relationships, the more likely they are to enjoy stable, healthy self-esteem.

Nostalgia pushes us toward sources of self-esteem that are better investments in the long term.

Think about it: If your self-esteem is inevitably influenced by social feedback and social approval, do you think it would be healthy and sustainable to focus on social connections that rely heavily on how attractive you are, how thin or muscular you are, how much status you have, what kind of car you drive, or how much money you make? Of course not. Unfortunately, extrinsic sources of self-esteem are seductive, so we need psychological resources that help us focus on intrinsic sources of self-esteem. Since nostalgia is more about intrinsic social relationships and a more authentic sense of self, it can help us resist the temptation of unhealthy and fragile sources of self-esteem and instead turn our efforts to more enriching and authentic sources of self-esteem. This reduces our concern about keeping up with the Joneses. In other words, nostalgia makes us less vulnerable to fixating on and chasing the types of social feedback and approval that might feel good in the moment but that ultimately distract us from deeper and more enduring social bonds.

Nostalgia doesn't just increase our self-esteem. Nostalgia pushes us toward sources of self-esteem that are better investments in the long term. When we engage in nostalgia, we don't tend to think about materialistic accomplishments. Instead, we focus on experiences connected with our most cherished relationships.

In one of my studies, a research participant described a nostalgic memory involving a birthday party he had as a child in which very few of the people he invited showed up. He noted that his feelings were hurt because he thought it meant that his classmates didn't like him. He had invited as many people as his parents would allow, but when only a handful showed up, he felt rejected. But then he and the few people who did attend ended up having a blast. This participant wrote that it took him years to fully appreciate the lesson from that experience—that what's truly important is having friends who genuinely want to spend time with you. He views this as an important nostalgic memory because it reminds him to focus on building and maintaining those types of sincere relationships and to prioritize quality over quantity when it comes to social life.

Even when our nostalgia involves consumer products (clothes and cars, for example), the connection to those things is often about something deeper. You might be nostalgic for the type of car you drove in high school because of the pleasant experiences you associate with it. Maybe you spent years saving for that car, making the purchase of it a landmark achievement that resulted from hard work and persistence. Or maybe you worked on fixing that car with your father, turning the car into a symbol of a cherished time spent with Dad. Maybe that car is associated with the sense of freedom you longed for as a young person as you were developing your identity.

Even when nostalgia appears to be superficial on the surface because it involves material possessions, if you dig a little deeper, you'll often find that the object is serving as a reminder of a more intrinsically fulfilling experience or set of experiences. People often collect things for this reason, even objects that are of little financial value to others. Most Americans (over 60 percent) consider themselves to be collectors.[7] Objects can help us contact cherished memories by serving as reminders of specific events and feelings from the past.

In one of my studies, a research participant shared a nostalgic memory about his comic-book collection. He joked about how he probably spends too much money as a grown man buying comic books (according to his wife, at least) but that he enjoys continuing to build his collection. It reminds him of the days he could spend hours in his bedroom reading and talking about comics with his older brother.

Do you have nostalgic feelings about certain material possessions? If so, take a few minutes to think about why those possessions are meaningful to you. I suspect you'll find that the objects that generate the most nostalgia aren't ones that reflect wealth or status but help you feel connected to family and close friends.

Nostalgia Makes You Less Defensive

Since self-esteem is so important to health and well-being, people are highly motivated to defend themselves when they feel it threatened. A large body of research documents the different self-defensive strategies people use to protect their self-esteem, including the tendency to attribute success to personal attributes and failure to external causes. When we fail or perform poorly, we're often tempted to respond by trying to minimize our culpability for the outcome and instead blame others or factors beyond our control. For example, an employee who receives a poor performance review might be tempted to blame the boss, unfavorable working conditions, bad company policy, or lousy coworkers, even if the poor performance was in fact the result of their own actions. Although this defensive tendency might seem to help protect our self-esteem, it actually makes it harder for us to learn from feedback and improve.

My colleagues and I wanted to find out if nostalgia might help people be more receptive to feedback. Because we worked at universities, we were aware that college students understandably like to think of themselves as generally smart, making any feedback that calls their intelligence into question a threat to their self-esteem. This gave us the opportunity to test if nostalgia would help college students be less defensive about their intelligence.[8]

In our study, we randomly assigned American college students to a difficult (negative feedback condition) or easy (positive feedback condition) purported test of analytic reasoning. They didn't know if they were receiving easy or hard questions. We did this so that students getting easy questions would get most of them right, making it easy for us to give them positive feedback (inform them they did better than the average student); and students receiving the difficult questions would get many of them wrong, making it easy for us to give them negative feedback (inform them they did worse than the average student).

After completing the test, these students were provided with a scoring key to allow them to see how they performed. The scoring key provided the correct answers to each question and, importantly, indicated how their score compared to other university students (scores of 0–4 were labeled "below average," 5–6 "average," and 7–10 "above average"). In reality, their scores were not related to any average. As planned, participants in the negative feedback condition scored in the below-average range for university students and those in the positive feedback group scored between the average to above-average range.

Nostalgia reduces the need to defend the self from negative feedback.

Next, participants were instructed either to write about a nostalgic or an ordinary experience. After this, they responded to the question "To what extent was your performance on the test caused by your ability?" Higher scores reflect a stronger internal (less defensive) attribution of performance. We predicted that since nostalgia boosts self-esteem, it would make students less defensive. The results supported this hypothesis. In the absence of nostalgia (i.e., the ordinary past condition), participants in the negative feedback condition were less likely to blame their own ability for their performance than participants in the positive feedback group.

This is a classic demonstration of *attribution bias*. People don't want to interpret negative feedback as their fault or as somehow reflective of their capabilities. However, nostalgia reduced this difference, making the students who were led to believe they performed below average take responsibility for their poor performance.

Nostalgia reduces the need to defend the self from negative feedback. Taking responsibility for outcomes we don't like allows us to move forward productively. Sometimes we aren't very good at something, and nondefensively accepting this fact can encourage us to explore other opportunities and goals that better fit our strengths. If we refuse to take critical feedback on board and instead blame external factors, we are more likely to find ourselves in situations in which we're just spinning our wheels or are constantly frustrated. Sometimes we have the potential to be good at something, but we fail to improve because of our stubborn defensiveness. Instead of being open to critique and learning from it, we dismiss useful feedback, make excuses, or even lash out at others.

By making us less defensive, nostalgia can help us improve, which ultimately leads to a healthier and stabler approach to self-esteem. In the short term, this might mean asking ourselves difficult questions about how we use our time and energy and whether we are as good at something as we'd like to imagine. In the long term, this makes it more likely that we invest our time and energy in the activities that make us more fulfilled.

Next time you receive critical feedback at work or in another area of life, reflect on how you're taking that feedback. If you find it difficult and find yourself becoming upset or defensive, try taking a step back and giving yourself an opportunity to open your mind to feedback. Nostalgia could help you in this regard. Spend a few minutes thinking about a nostalgic experience. How did it help you appreciate your value as a person? Once you remind yourself that you're someone with positive qualities, you might be better able to face critical feedback that might help you move forward with confidence.

Summary Notes for "Nostalgia Builds Healthy Self-Esteem"

- Different cultures pursue and express self-esteem in different ways. People all around the world value a positive view of self as well as the knowledge that they're meeting social and cultural standards.

- Too little self-esteem is associated with psychological and physical difficulties, whereas too much can make people narcissistic and uncaring.

- Nostalgia can help us cultivate healthy and sustainable sources of self-esteem, particularly those involving intrinsic social relationships—those with people who value us for our inherent characteristics.

- Nostalgia connects us to sources of self-esteem that are better investments in the long term and that make us less vulnerable to chasing the types of social feedback and approval that can distract us from more enduring social bonds.

- By making us less defensive, nostalgia encourages us to make the most of feedback and improve, which in turn leads to healthier self-esteem.

CHAPTER 6

NOSTALGIA HELPS THE SELF GROW AND EXPAND

When I was working on my PhD, I became fascinated with a philosophical debate happening within my general area of research on human motivation. I'll spare you the nerdier details, but the gist of the debate was on whether our motivation is more defense-oriented or growth-oriented. Are people more driven by the need to feel safe and secure or by the need to explore and grow?

On the defense side, scholars argue that the advanced intellectual capacities possessed by humans create a lot of anxiety, thus many of our attitudes and beliefs are about psychological threats and fears—death, physical pain and suffering, social rejection and loneliness, failure, uncertainty, meaninglessness, and so on. From this perspective, the self-concepts we develop and seek to affirm serve a self-protective function. As discussed in the previous chapter, people tend to blame others (or situations) for their failures, because blaming oneself is a threat to self-esteem. This suggests that our initial reaction to threat is self-defense. We prioritize protecting our self-concept over learning something that could help us grow as a person.

The scholars who hold this view propose that an organism must first have a good defense system in order to thrive. Without defense as the foundation of human psychology, people wouldn't be able to function; in fact, they'd be debilitated by insecurity and anxiety. Indeed, studies show that people with high self-esteem are less likely to experience anxiety in stressful situations than people with low self-esteem.[1]

In this research, self-esteem is viewed as a foundational defense mechanism that protects people from anxiety and helps them function in a world full of uncertainty and potential threats. If you've ever seen a visual representation of Maslow's hierarchy of needs, you have the basic idea: we humans need to meet more fundamental needs such as safety, belongingness, and self-esteem before we can approach the apogee of self-actualization.

On the other side of the debate, scholars argue that to suggest that psychological defense takes priority over psychological growth ignores the fact that from a very early age, humans are naturally curious and explorative, and being so is critical for cognitive, emotional, and social development. Infants and toddlers learn through experimentation and risk-taking. They're often fearless explorers who are driven to interact with the world around them as much as possible. From this perspective, the development of our self-concept (and learning in general) is an ongoing process rooted in our innate need for personal growth and self-expansion. Just as there are studies highlighting the ways self-defense appears to be fundamental to human psychology, there are also those that emphasize the importance of self-growth.

For example, studies find that people are more motivated to pursue a goal and feel a greater sense of self-esteem when pursuing it if they feel like the goal is motivated by their true self.[2] The true self—the self-concept people think most authentically characterizes them—is viewed by psychologists as growth-oriented because it isn't driven by external factors like social approval or material wealth. Instead, it's driven by the desire to reach our full potential.

The scholars on the self-growth side acknowledge that humans often engage in efforts to defend the self from fears and uncertainties, but they believe that self-growth takes priority. To them, self-defense is only triggered when people feel threatened, whereas the motive for self-growth is always active.

There are also scholars in this debate who believe that both self-defense and self-growth play an equally fundamental role in human motivation. I'm one of them. I call this the *dual motive* approach, the basic idea being that human motivation is a balancing act between defense and growth. For instance, infants naturally want to explore the world around them, but studies show that they're most willing to do so when there's a caregiver who makes them feel safe nearby.[3] This allows them to immediately access feelings of security if their explorative behavior causes them fear or pain.

This balancing act continues far beyond childhood. Adults are also motivated by both self-defense and self-growth and must regularly navigate the tension between these motives. Imagine you work for an advertising company and creativity is a big part of your job. You and your team are regularly tasked with developing novel marketing campaigns, which means you benefit from a work environment that fosters outside-the-box thinking. Now, imagine your work environment is tense and stressful. Your boss is punitive and harshly critical, and your coworkers are self-centered and unsupportive. You're anxious much of the time and constantly worry that your ideas will be ridiculed. Maybe you even worry that you'll be fired for putting forward an idea your boss doesn't like.

Security is clearly important for growth, but it can also be a barrier. Growth is essential, but it can sometimes undermine security.

Instead of that scenario, imagine a work environment that's supportive and inspiring. Your boss is kind and encouraging. Your coworkers are corroborative and generous with their time. You're happy much of the time at work, and you rarely worry that your ideas will be ridiculed or that you will be terminated for taking risks. Which of these environments do you think is more likely to foster outside-the-box thinking?

Just as infants and small children are more likely to explore, try new things, and take risks when they have the security that comes from loving caregivers, adults are more likely to do the same when they enjoy supportive family members, friends, managers, colleagues, and broader cultural institutions. Like children, adults naturally want to explore and grow, and this benefits individuals, organizations, and society as a whole. But adults also need psychological security, to feel like their lives make sense and that they're socially valued. And it isn't as simple as saying security comes first. Sometimes people start with a desire for growth—to create and innovate. However, such growth-oriented activities can lead to experiences that cause anxiety, uncertainty, and social disconnection, which reorients them toward security.

In addition, too much security can undermine growth. It seems obvious that you'll be more creative in a supportive environment than an unsupportive one, but what if your colleagues and supervisor are overly protective of your self-esteem and never give you the type of critical feedback that would help you take your work to the next level? Similarly, in the case of the curious child, what if parents and other caregivers always run to the rescue as soon as the child experiences any discomfort? Research finds that college students who say they had overcontrolling parents (helicopter parenting) are more likely to experience depression and less likely to feel confident in their abilities.[4]

Security is clearly important for growth, but it can also be a barrier. Growth is essential, but it can sometimes undermine security. The right balance of psychological defense and growth is critical to optimal functioning. In other words, defense and growth motives have a collaborative relationship—they work together in the service of human flourishing.

If self-defense and self-growth are both so critical, psychological resources that support the balance between them should be uniquely beneficial. Nostalgia is such a resource.

Nostalgia Helps You Pursue Self-Growth by Meeting Self-Defense Needs

Personal growth involves change. Some of the time, growth-promoting change isn't distressing and is in fact quite pleasant. Imagine you're trying to figure out something to watch on Netflix and you come across a documentary about the history of different types of food around the world. You decide to give it a shot and, as a result, you learn something new about Indian Chinese cuisine. Perhaps this even inspires you to experiment with new recipes. This might sound like an insignificant step toward personal growth, but over time these types of steps accumulate to expand your horizons and help you become a worldlier and more interesting person. Who knows, maybe watching that food documentary was the initial spark that led you down a path toward a new hobby or career.

Personal growth would be easy if it relied entirely on pleasant experiences. Sometimes to grow and improve our lives and the lives of others, we need to face hardship, criticism, self-doubt, uncertainty, stress, and loneliness. But these distressing states can undermine growth by causing us to become defensive.

Nostalgia helps us manage the unpleasant experiences associated with growth so we don't get derailed by the need for self-defense. I've talked to many adults who've decided to change careers for a variety of reasons. Some became burned out and wanted to try something different to improve their mental health. Some never liked their former career to begin with; it didn't reflect their true self. They pursued it because it seemed practical at the time—it was accessible and would meet their financial needs. But eventually they arrived in a position to try a career path that better reflected what they're most passionate about.

Regardless the reason for the change, the move wasn't easy. It meant giving up a reliable paycheck for less stable income, or it involved going back to school—often with people much younger and more comfortable with current technology. Or it meant working in a new organizational structure that meant losing their seniority. Or it involved moving to a new city where they didn't know anyone. In such situations, nostalgia can be a critical resource.

Consider the above example of having to learn new technological skills. When I was a college professor, I occasionally had nontraditional students in my classes. Young students are often referred to as *digital natives*—they grew up in the information age. People my age and older remember a time without the internet, but most of my students don't. They've gained a considerable amount of experience using different software platforms throughout their education and in everyday life. For them, an assignment that involves creating digital media isn't a big deal, but an older student might find the same assignment quite stressful if they haven't had a lot of experience creating digital content. You can imagine an older student feeling like they're behind the ball, that it's too late for them to catch up. This might lead them to believe they'd be better off dropping out of college, that their new career goal doesn't fit their self-concept. This is just one way that personal growth can be sabotaged by defensive thinking.

Dozens of studies find that negative psychological states that tend to orient people away from growth and toward defense make people become more nostalgic.[5] Critically, nostalgia meets defense needs so people can continue to focus on growth. Remember the discussion on self-continuity in chapter 4? When people face life experiences that cause self-discontinuity, they become more nostalgic, which restores feelings of self-continuity. This allows them to continue moving forward and not get derailed by the distressing state of self-discontinuity.

Nostalgia offers people a way to manage psychological threats that undermine growth motivation.

A nontraditional student feeling out of place in college is an example of a situation that could cause the type of self-discontinuity that might tempt the student to drop out in a defensive effort to regain feelings of self-continuity. But if nostalgia helps restore self-continuity, it can help the student avoid the temptation to drop out and remain focused on their self-growth goal of finishing the college degree program.

Helping people maintain self-continuity is just one way nostalgia contributes to balancing self-defense and self-growth. More broadly, nostalgia offers people a way to manage psychological threats that undermine growth motivation. By increasing different forms of well-being such as self-continuity and self-esteem (particularly when people experience stress and uncertainty), nostalgia makes it easier for us to keep moving forward in the pursuit of learning something new, expanding our horizons, and achieving our goals.

We can view nostalgia as a substitute for the types of psychological defenses that undermine growth. Imagine receiving negative feedback at work. To defend your self-esteem, instead of taking the feedback to heart and looking for ways to improve, you blame others. What if, instead, you managed your self-esteem by reflecting nostalgically on experiences that point out your positive qualities? The nostalgic memories help you see the bigger picture and remind you that your current experience doesn't reflect who you are as a whole. This takes the sting out of your current situation, which makes it easier to view the feedback as information that can help you improve. In this way, nostalgia can offer a more positive way to defend the self than methods that might ultimately get in the way of becoming better at your job.

One way to use nostalgia in such situations is to make a list of challenges you're facing that might trigger the need for psychological defense. These can be problems at work or home, specific goals you're working on that involve receiving feedback or experiencing failure, or any other issues you're dealing with that might call up stress, anxiety, uncertainty, self-doubt, or other unpleasant emotional states. Looking at your list, think of any nostalgic memories that might help you affirm yourself so that you can better navigate each of these challenges in ways that allow you to remain open to critical feedback and learn from your mistakes and failures.

Nostalgia Promotes Self-Confidence by Reminding You of Past Self-Growth

When people engage in nostalgic reflection, they often recall experiences that involve examples of personal growth. It can be helpful (but not necessary) if we have nostalgic memories that are directly related to our present problems. For instance, when someone is dealing with stress at work, it's useful to bring to mind nostalgic experiences involving work because it makes the connection from past to present more evident.

As previously noted, nostalgia can promote growth by offering a substitution for self-defense. We considered the case of receiving negative feedback in an evaluation at work. Imagine if the nostalgic memory you reflected on to protect your self-esteem in response to that critique involved a past professional accomplishment you were proud of. This could help you respond to the negative evaluation with the belief that, based on past successes, you have the present and future ability to succeed. Nostalgia did more than help protect your self-esteem; it served as a guide for self-improvement.

Nostalgia doesn't have to be directly relevant to current challenges to be helpful for overcoming them. Even a nostalgic memory that seems relatively trivial—taking a road trip with friends, for example—involves examples of personal accomplishment that can promote self-growth in other areas of life.

In one of my studies, a research participant described riding across America on his motorcycle with a couple of friends. They encountered various challenges on the trip—hitting unfavorable weather, getting lost, running low on money, and experiencing mechanical problems. Part of what made the trip so memorable was having to overcome these hardships. It brought the friends closer together and demonstrated to the participant that when push came to shove, he could rely on his resourcefulness to get out of a tough spot. He was able to adapt and find solutions to diverse challenges. We can all access such memories to foster self-growth when facing uncertainty and self-doubt.

On the surface, a nostalgic memory about a cross-country motorcycle trip has little to do with something like the stress of going back to college as a middle-aged adult and struggling to keep up with new technology. But such a memory can be quite helpful because it has the power to remind us that we've been in difficult spots before and were able to successfully navigate them.

Indeed, my colleagues and I have found that nostalgia increases general self-confidence and optimism.[6] For example, in studies in which participants spent a few minutes writing about a nostalgic or an ordinary past memory and then completed a questionnaire measuring how optimistic they were about their futures, those who wrote about the nostalgic memory were more likely to view their future optimistically than those who wrote about an ordinary memory. Regardless of what our nostalgic memories entail, they have the ability to promote a growth-oriented mindset.

Think about a growth goal you're currently pursuing or would like to pursue. This could be a professional goal, but it could also be personal or social. What's the biggest barrier to achieving your goal? Are you holding back in any way out of fear or worry? Now bring to mind a nostalgic memory that involves a personal accomplishment or a time when you triumphed over hardship. What specific personal strengths does this memory reveal about you? How might you use those strengths to help with your current goal? If it's difficult to make a connection between your nostalgic memories and your current challenges, it can be helpful to write about the memory. As part of this exercise, try to specifically describe what the memory reveals about your capacity for resilience and growth.

Nostalgia Increases Creativity

Nostalgia also supports self-growth by encouraging creative expression. Creativity involves outside-the-box thinking. When we engage in creative activities, we're expressing ourselves in new ways, and that expands the self. Nostalgia inspires creativity in two distinct ways: it meets our defensive needs and it enhances our passion.

As discussed before, anxiety and fear can be barriers to growth. Creativity involves risk-taking, and it's hard to take risks when we're distressed or afraid. Some of my earliest research focused on this issue. I found that people are most able to be creative when they're anxious if they focus their attention on something that makes them feel more secure (such as their family and friends).

Think back to my example of the company in which employees would be more likely to think outside the box if they worked in a socially supportive environment. Even when people enjoy an encouraging work setting, they might still face self-generated barriers to creativity. Despite supportive feedback, some people worry their ideas aren't good enough. Maybe they worry about a lot of things most of the time. Maybe they're experiencing problems with family or friends that are creating undue stress and anxiety. In such situations, nostalgia can serve as an additional resource. Nostalgia offers people a way to self-regulate. Revisiting cherished experiences is a restorative activity that reduces stress and boosts positive mood. This makes it easier to focus one's energy on being creative.

Nostalgia also inspires creativity by giving people a reason to want to be creative. We are more likely to take risks and express ourselves in original ways when we feel passionate about the project we're working on. Nostalgia focuses our energy on something we care deeply about because nostalgia is about personally cherished memories.

People regularly use nostalgia as a foundation for creativity. Screenwriters and directors regularly mention movies they watched as children or young adults as sources of inspiration. Their nostalgia helps them reconnect with the emotions they experienced early in life that made them love movies. Often they have specific memories of films that motivate them to want to create the type of work that will have a similar effect on moviegoers today. The same is true for musicians. They'll share how the songs they heard growing up inspired their music. A lot of creative expression is simply taking something old and adding a new twist or reimagining it in a way that feels more applicable to the modern world. For example, the filmmaker Quentin Tarantino is well known for applying his nostalgia for films from diverse cultures and subcultures to make works that are both extremely creative and a tribute to the old movies he loves. His *Kill Bill* movies are a clever combination of samurai, kung fu, and western films.

Most of us aren't Hollywood filmmakers or famous musicians, but we have creative passions that are fueled by nostalgia. For several years

I've worked as a consultant for a major scrapbooking company. When people create scrapbooks, they aren't simply cataloging memories. Like a filmmaker or writer, they're using their creative energy to tell stories—stories that are personally important to them that they often want to share with others. The scrapbooking process offers a way to interact with nostalgic memories, arrange specific themes, and produce something they can revisit and pass down to future generations. Many scrapbookers think of themselves as responsible for preserving family memories and traditions, and their nostalgia drives the creative process that makes this possible.

Research supports the idea that nostalgia inspires creativity. In one study conducted by Shengquan Ye and his colleagues at the City University of Hong Kong, university students were randomly assigned to write about a nostalgic experience or describe their schedule and activities from the previous day.[7] To assess creativity, participants were given a task that involved generating a list of possible uses for three common objects. Specifically, they were instructed to think of and list as many possible uses they could think of for a brick, a shoe, and a newspaper. Participants were given three minutes per object. Researchers totaled the number of generated ideas and used this score as an indicator of fluency of creativity. Participants in the nostalgia condition generated more uses of common objects than did participants in the control condition.

Nostalgia helps people express themselves creatively because it makes people more open to new and risky ideas.

Another series of studies conducted by Wijnand A. P. van Tilburg, a psychology professor at the University of Essex, and a team of researchers at the University of Southampton examined nostalgia's impact on creativity, as well as the mindset that makes creativity more likely.[8] In one study, research participants spent a few minutes writing about a nostalgic or ordinary past experience. Next, they were asked to write a short story that began with "One cold winter evening, a man and a woman were alarmed by a sound coming from a nearby house." The researchers found that participants who wrote about a nostalgic experience also generated short stories that were judged to be far more creative.

In another study, researchers had participants complete a questionnaire measuring openness to new ideas.[9] This included items such as "I see myself as someone who is inventive" and "I see myself as someone who has an active imagination." They also had participants complete a questionnaire asking them the extent to which they approach challenging tasks by trying to be creative and risk-taking or by relying on safe and familiar solutions. The researchers found that participants in the nostalgia condition scored significantly higher on openness to new ideas than participants in the control condition. Nostalgia participants also expressed a greater preference for using creativity and risk-taking in the face of challenges. These findings suggest that nostalgia helps people express themselves creatively because it makes people more open to new and risky ideas. Nostalgia promotes creative cognition.

> What are some hobbies or activities you enjoy or would like to pursue that offer the chance to explore new ideas or experiences? If you're struggling to come up with ideas, a trip down memory lane can help. When you were younger, what sparked your imagination? What made you feel most creative? How can you use those experiences to inspire creativity in the present?

In one of my studies, a research participant shared a nostalgic memory involving an experience she had in her early twenties when she was a vocalist for an indie rock band. She described how she never imagined herself as the type of person who would go on stage and perform in front of a live audience even though she enjoyed writing music and singing. But then she was encouraged by a close friend who played guitar in the band to try being the band's lead singer after the former one had abruptly quit. The participant reluctantly said yes even though she was terrified. Her nostalgic memory was about the first time she performed live with the band. It was at a small bar, and there were only a couple dozen people in the audience, but that night was when she truly discovered a creative passion for performance art. She noted that the band didn't last very long, but looking back on that first experience nearly two decades ago made her want to find new ways to get back in touch with her creative side and do something once again that allowed her to push herself outside of her comfort zone.

Nostalgia is a crucial resource for the self. It helps us figure out who we are, and it increases our self-esteem and self-confidence. Additionally, it orients us toward personal growth. When you're stuck in a rut, unsure which direction to take in life, and you need a fresh way to expand your horizons or seek creative inspiration, try looking to the past. Your nostalgic memories are a treasure chest of experiences you've collected over the course of your life that are always there to aid in your personal growth.

Summary Notes for "Nostalgia Helps the Self Grow and Expand"

- Human motivation is an ongoing balancing act between our needs for security and growth. We need the right balance between these for optimal functioning.

- By fostering self-continuity and self-esteem, nostalgia empowers us to pursue our desires, face new challenges, and achieve our goals.

- No matter what our nostalgic memories are about, they have the potential to promote self-growth.

- Revisiting valued memories helps reduce stress and improve our mood, which in turn boosts creativity.

- Nostalgia encourages us to open our minds and engage in outside-the-box thinking.

PART 3

HOW NOSTALGIA CONNECTS YOU TO OTHERS

CHAPTER 7

NOSTALGIA STRENGTHENS AND BUILDS RELATIONSHIPS

Thanks to advances in technology, it's extremely easy for humans to connect with each other. And yet in many ways we're becoming more socially disconnected. In 2018, the prime minister of the United Kingdom appointed a minister of loneliness in response to growing concerns about mental and physical health problems among British people. Indeed, a 2017 survey found that roughly 14 percent of the British population indicated that they often (or always) felt lonely.[1]

The problem is potentially worse in the United States. A similar survey in 2018 revealed that 22 percent of US citizens said they often or always feel lonely, and this was a couple of years before COVID-19 hit. A 2021 survey conducted by Harvard University found that 36 percent of Americans (and 61 percent of young adults) experienced serious loneliness during the pandemic.[2] Other surveys further paint a depressing picture of present-day social life. According to the Survey Center for American Life, in 1990, only 2 percent of American women and 3 percent of American men reported having no friends. In 2021, these numbers increased to 10 percent for women and 15 percent for men.[3]

Loneliness is often viewed as a problem specific to the elderly. Certainly older adults have unique challenges associated with retirement, declining mobility and health, and the death of family members and similarly aged friends. People are also living longer and having fewer children, which means that older adults may lack family support systems in the future.

Emerging research indicates that loneliness is increasingly a problem for younger generations as well. Today's teenagers and young adults spend less time engaged in in-person social activities with friends than those of past generations.[4] They're also lonelier. A 2019 YouGov survey revealed that among millennials, 25 percent reported having no acquaintances, 22 percent said they had no friends, 27 percent claimed they had no close friends, and 30 percent said they didn't have best friends.[5]

The causes of our growing loneliness are fiercely debated and undoubtedly complex. Individualism, economic affluence, the decline of religion, and the rise of electronic and social media have all been blamed and are likely interrelated. For instance, the wealthier a society becomes, the more people can live on their own and pursue individual interests. In many ways, this type of financial and social freedom is desirable, but it can also weaken social ties.

I'll spend more time on the challenges of electronic entertainment and social media in part 5 of this book, but for now I'll just note that it isn't only young people who are spending much of their free time on the internet. The paradox is that the more technology offers us ways to stay connected to loved ones and form new relationships with others all over the world, we're somehow becoming lonelier and lonelier.

Loneliness isn't just a form of social suffering. It contributes to a large number of mental and physical health problems. Loneliness is a major risk factor for depression, suicide, and cognitive decline. Loneliness makes people perceive their lives as meaningless. Loneliness is also associated with poor sleep, elevated blood pressure, and weakened immunity. Chronic loneliness—feeling lonely for long periods of time—has been linked to deaths caused by cancer and cardiovascular disease.[6]

To get a sense of how important social connection is to health, a group of researchers led by Julianne Holt-Lunstad, a professor of psychology and neuroscience at Brigham Young University, combined a collection of large data sets that allowed them to examine the association between social disconnection and mortality. They found that social isolation, loneliness, and living alone increased the likelihood of death between 26 and 32 percent over a seven-year period.[7]

Loneliness and other forms of social disconnection are harmful to mental and physical health because humans are a highly social species. We have a basic need to belong. A good portion of our attention and thinking is focused on observing, understanding, and navigating the social world—what psychologists refer to as *social cognition*.

Think about how much of your day involves interacting with others or planning for interactions with them. You might work in a profession that doesn't seem particularly social, but would your job exist without clients or customers? Outside of work, how much of your time do you spend with other people? How often do you engage in activities that impact other people?

Nearly everything we do connects us to each other. Even when we watch television, listen to podcasts, or play video games by ourselves, we're also consuming or interacting with media about people.

Our sociality starts at birth. Infants are helpless without adult caregivers, and children and adolescents require parents, older family members, teachers, and other mentors to become healthy adults. The success of our species is the result of our ability to build personal relationships and larger groups in the service of pursuing shared goals that advance community and allow individuals to reach their full potential.

Given the critical role that sociality plays in human development and flourishing, it shouldn't be surprising that social disconnection is harmful to well-being and health. It's also not surprising that people have psychological resources (like nostalgia) they can deploy to restore or build new relationships when they experience disconnection.

Social Disconnection Makes You Nostalgic

People often think of nostalgia as being caused by experiences that explicitly remind us of the past. For example, hearing an old song or seeing images related to our past activates old memories. This is what advertisers who use nostalgia to sell products are counting on. Nostalgia-oriented marketing directly focuses our attention on good feelings we associate with the past. Social interactions are also common triggers. When we run into old friends or gather with our families for the holidays, nostalgic memories tend to follow.

My colleagues and I were interested in less obvious nostalgia triggers. It makes sense that hearing an old song, being exposed to certain advertisements, or hanging out with high school friends would increase nostalgic feelings. We wanted to know if there are internal psychological states that make people feel nostalgic.

The first thing we discovered was that people are far more likely to become nostalgic when they experience negative emotions rather than positive ones. In one early study, we asked research participants to reflect on and describe the circumstances in which they tend to become nostalgic.[8] Experiences involving negative emotions were the most frequently mentioned circumstances leading to nostalgia; nearly 40 percent indicated that they typically feel nostalgic when they're in a negative mood. Only 3 percent reported becoming nostalgic when they were feeling positive. Other studies revealed the same results. In one, we had research participants read news stories that were depressing, uplifting, or emotionally neutral and then administered a questionnaire concerning how nostalgic they felt in the moment. We found that people felt significantly more nostalgic after reading the depressing news. In addition, loneliness was the most frequently cited negative emotional state to trigger nostalgia among research participants.

Based on this finding, we wanted to more systematically test the idea that loneliness triggers nostalgia. Just because people say they tend to be nostalgic when they feel lonely doesn't mean that loneliness causes nostalgia. In fact, it could mean that nostalgia makes people feel lonely because it reminds them of past relationships they no longer have or social experiences they can't recreate. We needed a different experiment to determine if enhanced loneliness would cause people to become nostalgic.

But how does one induce loneliness? Certainly it would be unethical, not to mention impractical, to manipulate people's lives in a way that would create severe loneliness. Fortunately, psychological researchers don't have to do something as drastic as harming people's social lives to experimentally test how loneliness impacts them. Instead, researchers use techniques that allow them to test their ideas with temporary and minor inductions of negative experiences such as loneliness. We used one of these techniques.

We took advantage of the fact that all adults have, at some point in their lives, felt at least a little bit lonely. In other words, people understand the basic experience of loneliness. Even the most socially blessed among us occasionally deal with it. We recruited students at a British university and randomly assigned them to two groups: a high-loneliness group and a low-loneliness group. To create these, we had participants fill out a questionnaire, but we altered the questionnaire for each group. For participants randomly assigned to the high-loneliness group, we phrased the items in the questionnaire to elicit general agreement (e.g., "I *sometimes* feel isolated from others"). Since everyone likely feels lonely at least occasionally, most people would agree with such statements. For the randomly assigned participants in the low-loneliness group, we worded the prompts to encourage general disagreement (e.g., "I *always* feel isolated from others"). Thankfully most people don't feel lonely all the time, so very few people will likely agree with such statements.

In other words, we used the same questionnaire for both groups but framed the response options so that research participants would generally agree or disagree with the items of the questionnaire. This helped set up the next part of the experiment: We gave participants feedback intended to temporally enhance or decrease loneliness. Participants were told that the experimenter was scoring their questionnaire in order to provide them with feedback, which was then offered on a form. Participants in the high-loneliness group were informed that they had scored high (in the 62nd percentile) on the loneliness inventory. Participants in the low-loneliness group were told that they had scored low (in the 12th percentile) on loneliness. Again, this feedback was made more believable because of the way we had worded the questionnaires that provided the basis for this feedback. After receiving this feedback, participants were asked to complete questions about how nostalgic they currently felt. This is how we found that loneliness increased nostalgia. Participants in the high-loneliness group reported statistically significant higher levels of nostalgia than participants in the low-loneliness group. Other studies (including one in China—a culture quite different from the study of British participants mentioned above) found similar results.[9]

When people imagine social disconnection in their future, they're more likely to experience nostalgia.

When researchers perform these types of studies, they inform participants about the details of the experiment as soon as it is over. This is known as debriefing. This means our participants didn't leave the laboratory convinced that they were lonelier than the average person. We also discussed with participants why such experiments are important and gave them the opportunity to ask questions. If anything, the participants left with the encouraging message that they'd played a role in helping researchers better understand a serious problem such as loneliness.

Of course, loneliness in real life, especially chronic loneliness, isn't the same as being made to feel a little lonely for a short period of time in a research laboratory. But experiments like the one described above are important for establishing causal relationships. The fact that researchers can trigger nostalgia with a subtle and harmless loneliness induction suggests that longer-lasting and more severe loneliness is a powerful trigger of nostalgia. Indeed, the results of our experiments are consistent with surveys that reveal that people who frequently experience loneliness in their lives report feeling nostalgic more often than those who don't report the same level of loneliness.[10]

In a related study, my colleagues and I recruited young American adults to complete a personality assessment, informing half of them that based on their specific personality, they were more likely to experience relationship failures in the future. The other half were informed that their personality type was predictive of relationship success.[11] We found that those presented with a more pessimistic social outlook became significantly more nostalgic than the other group. When people imagine social disconnection in their future, they're more likely to experience nostalgia.

Nostalgia Makes You Feel More Socially Connected

Just because loneliness and other forms of social disconnection make people nostalgic doesn't mean that nostalgia is good for them. It could be that nostalgia only makes people feel more socially disconnected. Most nostalgic memories are social. Perhaps when people feel socially disconnected, they long for a time when they felt connected, but since that past is long gone, nostalgia makes them feel even worse than they already feel. This would suggest that not only does social disconnection cause nostalgia but that nostalgia causes feelings of disconnection.

My colleagues and I first tested this possibility with an experiment in which we recruited research participants from a British university and randomly assigned them to spend a few minutes writing about a nostalgic or an ordinary life experience.[12] They then completed questionnaires that measured mood and feelings of social connectedness. If nostalgia makes people feel worse, it should increase negative emotions, but that's not what we found. Reflecting on a nostalgic experience is more likely to make people feel happy than sad.

> Nostalgia doesn't make people feel worse; it makes them feel better.

This doesn't mean that nostalgia is pure joy. Nostalgic memories are emotionally complex or bittersweet, often involving a feeling of loss. Even so, there are now dozens of studies examining how reflecting on these memories impacts emotional states, and the general conclusion is that nostalgia is more sweet than bitter.[13] The recognition of loss doesn't cause emotional distress in the present. Instead, it often makes people feel grateful for that time. Even if it is accompanied with a tinge of sadness, that sadness is commonly overshadowed by the positive emotions associated with nostalgia. In other words, nostalgia doesn't make people feel worse; it makes them feel better.

In the same study, we asked participants to rate their agreement with statements such as "Thinking about this event makes me feel loved." Those who reflected on a nostalgic memory didn't feel less socially connected than those who wrote about an ordinary memory. The opposite was the case—nostalgia made people feel more socially connected.

Since that original experiment, my colleagues and I (along with other researchers) have conducted dozens of studies in countries around the world examining the effect of nostalgia on social connectedness by employing different methods to induce nostalgia.[14] We've had participants listen to music that makes them nostalgic or music they enjoy that doesn't have much of a connection to their past. We've had participants watch nostalgic or non-nostalgic YouTube videos. We've had participants read fictional stories that include or do not include nostalgia-inducing content. In all these studies, the pattern remains the same: nostalgia fosters a sense of connection.

Why does revisiting cherished memories make people feel connected in the present? There are a number of reasons. For one, nostalgia reinforces long-distance connections. In my nearly twenty years as a college professor, I frequently encountered first-year students who struggled to adjust to college because they'd moved away from home and everyone they knew. The first semester is often tough, especially for students who are shy and have a difficult time forming new relationships. It's easy for them to feel alone, and this feeling can make them forget that there are people in their lives who care about them. Nostalgia reminds them of this fact. It encourages them to look beyond their immediate struggles to see a broader social picture. It gives them comfort to remember that their current experience doesn't represent the full picture of their lives. Understanding this can make their current state of loneliness less painful.

For example, in one of my studies, a student in her first year of college reflected on a nostalgic memory about skiing in Montana with her family when she was a child. She noted that most of her family still lived in Montana but that she wanted to go to college out of state (but not too far away, which is why she decided to attend a school in North Dakota). She wrote that she enjoyed thinking about the skiing memory because it reminded her that even when she felt alone, she had family back home who loved her.

Research examining how nostalgia helps people cope with loneliness offers empirical support for my experience with these college students. A team of researchers led by Xinyue Zhou at Zhejiang University in China found that nostalgia helps people cope with loneliness.[15] More specifically, these researchers discovered that loneliness makes people feel like they don't have social support, and that that loneliness increases nostalgia, which in turn restores feelings of social support. Nostalgia reminds lonely individuals that there are people out there who care.

In a more recent study, Zhou and her colleagues observed that nostalgia helped people in China, the United States, and the UK cope with the negative emotions caused by loneliness during the COVID-19 pandemic.[16] Another study conducted in Mexico during the pandemic by Rogelio Puente-Diaz, a professor of business and economics at Anahuac Mexico Norte, and his research team found that nostalgia increased a sense of belongingness.[17]

Even subtle nostalgia cues reinforce feelings of social connectedness. In one study, Chelsea A. Reid, a psychology professor at the College of Charleston, and her colleagues exposed participants to different scents.[18] They found that when people smell something that makes them feel nostalgic, they feel more loved and connected to others. This helps explain why we find certain smells to be comforting, even those that might not normally be considered pleasant.

As a kid, I spent many summers mowing lawns with my dad. Even now, the smell of gasoline triggers memories of that time, which I find especially meaningful since my dad is no longer alive. It isn't that I like the smell of gasoline. I don't. But it makes me nostalgic for time with my dad, which are memories I enjoy. Of course, many of the scents that evoke nostalgia are pleasant, such as the smell of different foods we associate with family gatherings for holidays and other traditions.

Another reason nostalgia boosts feelings of social connectedness is because it makes people more optimistic. This helps individuals who might currently feel socially disconnected have a broader view beyond their current struggles. Several studies show that after people engage in nostalgic reflection, they feel more optimistic about their future, and this includes optimism about their future social lives.[19]

My colleague Andrew Abeyta, a professor of psychology at Rutgers University-Camden, and I have investigated nostalgia's influence on social optimism. In one study, we asked some participants to write about an experience that makes them nostalgic or an ordinary life experience.[20] After that, as part of a separate questionnaire, they answered questions concerning how optimistic they were about achieving relationship goals in the future. Research participants who wrote about a nostalgic experience were significantly more optimistic than those who wrote about an ordinary experience.

Studies such as these offer evidence that nostalgia is often a future-oriented experience. When people nostalgically reflect on past experiences shared with loved ones, they not only feel more socially connected in the present but they also imagine a socially fulfilling future.

For example, in one of the studies my colleagues and I conducted, a participant shared a memory about attending her grandson's birthday party. She wrote that her daughter and son-in-law lived far away, so she didn't get to see them as much as she would like to. However, she was able to visit them around the time of her grandson's tenth birthday and was able to participate in his party. Of note, she wrote that it's often easy for her to feel down and disconnected but that thinking about this memory lifted her spirits and made her more optimistic about being able to spend more time with her children and grandchildren in the future.

Bring to mind a nostalgic experience that involves cherished time spent with a loved one. Spend a few minutes thinking deeply about this memory. You could also write about the memory or look at old photos or videos that capture or remind you of it. Try repeating this activity several times, bringing to mind and reflecting on a number of social nostalgic memories. Use these activities to remind yourself of your social bonds and why they're important to you. Such activities can be especially useful when you're stressed, feeling down, or are dealing with relationship challenges.

Nostalgia Motivates You to Connect

It's easy to imagine that nostalgia could be a barrier to creating and maintaining a healthy social life. If nostalgia reduces the pain of loneliness of new college students by focusing their mind on memories shared with friends and family back home, might it also reduce the likelihood that they feel motivated to make new friends? Instead of dwelling on past social bonds, shouldn't they be focused on creating new ones?

Lonely students should seek new friendships. One of the many benefits of attending college is the opportunity to meet new people from different places. But nostalgia isn't a roadblock to doing so; it's a resource that supports social goals. As already noted, nostalgia makes people more socially optimistic about the future. In another study Andrew Abeyta and I conducted, we found that when people feel pessimistic about their social lives, they become more nostalgic.[21] People can use nostalgia to restore an optimistic outlook about their future social lives.

We also found that nostalgia increases *social efficacy*—confidence in our ability to find and maintain relationships. This makes sense if you think about the content of nostalgic memories because most of them involve examples of social success. When people nostalgically reflect on experiences that highlight their social achievements, they're better able to see a path forward through current relationship difficulties. Nostalgia inspires both optimism and self-confidence.

More broadly, research indicates that nostalgia encourages people to prioritize social goals.[22] Life can get busy; it's easy to neglect even our most important relationships. But nostalgia focuses our attention back on them. Just as nostalgia helps you focus on your true self, it helps you focus on the relationships that support your social health.

Nostalgia generates the type of optimism and confidence needed to create and maintain close relationships, even when those relationships are under stress.

Andrew Abeyta and I also wanted to test if nostalgia could help nurture the type of mindset that's oriented toward solving relationship problems. Sometimes social suffering isn't the result of not having social contacts but instead occurs because people experience social conflict. They fight with family or friends, which makes them feel disconnected and socially stressed out.

To see if nostalgia could be useful in helping people resolve social conflicts, we conducted a study in which we first had participants listen to music that made them feel nostalgic or music that wasn't associated with nostalgic memories.[23] Next, participants completed a friendship conflict task. They were asked to bring to mind their best friend and were then given the following instructions:

> Now imagine that you and your close friend got into a disagreement. You and your friend have tried to resolve this conflict but things just are not the same. You have noticed that since the disagreement, you hang out less often. When you do see your friend, he or she seems a bit cold and distant. Sure, your friend is nice enough and you get along, but it is clear that this disagreement has driven a wedge between you.

After completing this task, participants were asked a series of questions concerning how much they would dedicate themselves to resolving the problem and how optimistic they were that they could do so. We found that participants who listened to nostalgic music were more dedicated to resolving the conflict and more optimistic they could resolve it. Nostalgia doesn't just make people feel connected. Nostalgia generates the type of optimism and confidence needed to create and maintain close relationships, even when those relationships are under stress.

Creating and maintaining social bonds requires more than the right mindset. It takes action. People need to go out and interact with others. Therefore, in our research on how nostalgia influences social life, Andrew Abeyta and I also wanted to test if nostalgia makes people more inclined to engage in social behavior. We were especially interested in social engagement with strangers because it involves a certain amount of social risk-taking. Most people probably wouldn't be surprised to learn that nostalgia makes us want to interact with existing friends and family, especially if our nostalgic memory involves them. However, building new relationships requires us to interact with people who aren't implicated in our nostalgia.

We hypothesized that nostalgia would motivate people to interact with strangers because nostalgia increases social efficacy. Nostalgia gives people the type of confidence that's useful for taking social risks, for putting ourselves out there. In addition, we believed that the more people's nostalgia focuses on past social experiences, the more it will inspire them to engage in behavior that paves the way for new relationships.

To test this, we first administered a questionnaire in which individuals indicated how nostalgic they felt about twenty different aspects of their past. Some of these were highly social (friends, family, people they loved) and some less so (music, toys, not having to worry so much). To be clear, things such as music and childhood toys can certainly be linked to relationships; they just aren't as explicitly social as friends and family. Our idea was that higher levels of nostalgia would lead to more social engagement but that this connection would be especially strong for nostalgia that's markedly social.

After participants completed this questionnaire, they were informed that we wanted to gauge interest in future research studies we planned to conduct. We then provided them with a description of four different studies they could participate in. The first two were titled "Personality and Social Interaction" and "Solving Problems with Others," and their descriptions indicated that participants would be interacting with other people as part of the studies. The remaining two studies were more nonsocial ("Cognitive Problem Solving" and "Personality and Opinions about Music"). The descriptions of these latter two studies indicated that participants would work alone.

In general, the more people reported feeling nostalgic about different aspects of their past, the more they were interested in participating in a study that involved interacting with others. Nostalgia was not, however, related to interest in participating in studies that didn't involve social interaction. In other words, nostalgia didn't make people want to partake in being a research participant in just any study; it specifically made them interested in studies that offered the opportunity to meet and interact with others. In addition, we observed that it was nostalgia that was high in sociality that drove people's interest in opportunities to meet and connect with others. Nostalgia doesn't just make people want to reconnect with old friends or work to strengthen existing relationships; it encourages them to be more outgoing and more interested in meeting new people.

Nostalgia makes us feel connected and socially confident.

As another way to determine if nostalgia pushes people to be more social, we had Chinese college students write about a nostalgic or an ordinary experience.[24] Next, they were informed that as part of the study, they would have a brief conversation with another person participating in the study. Participants were then asked to help prepare the room for the social interaction by setting up a couple of chairs in the room while the experimenter went to get the other participant. After each participant placed the chairs, the experimenter returned to the room and measured the distance between the chairs. If nostalgia promotes sociality, we predicted that those asked to reflect on an experience of nostalgia would place the chairs closer together than those in the control condition. And that's exactly what we found. When people feel nostalgic, they want to be physically closer to others.

Nostalgia makes us feel connected and socially confident. It motivates us to pursue our social goals and work to solve relationship problems. It even pushes us physically toward others. Nostalgia amplifies our social nature.

> If you're experiencing difficulty with your social motivation, try spending some time engaging in nostalgic reflection or in activities that make you feel nostalgic. This might help you get out of a funk and back in the social game.

Why Nostalgia Is Especially Helpful for Combating Loneliness

I've briefly described a number of studies that show how nostalgia energizes social life in various ways. These studies are at odds with the view that nostalgia keeps people focused on the past and is thus a barrier to cultivating a healthy social life in the present and future. Nostalgia is a way for people to draw strength and inspiration from past social experiences. This makes us feel socially supported, optimistic, and confident—and this pushes us toward others.

In this way, we can think of nostalgia as a general social resource for anyone needing a little inspiration. This is wonderful, but I also want to emphasize how important nostalgia is for combating loneliness in particular. Loneliness is problematic, in part, because it's self-reinforcing. Loneliness leads to more loneliness. The lonelier people feel, the less socially competent they perceive themselves to be and the more likely they are to withdraw from others. This makes it difficult for lonely people to restore relationships or form new ones. Since loneliness causes psychological suffering and is a risk factor for a number of mental and physical health problems, it's critical to identify resources that can help people respond to loneliness in ways that won't compound their loneliness.

Based on our previous findings, Andrew Abeyta and I endeavored to further test nostalgia's potential to short-circuit the maladaptive mental states that loneliness creates. Remember, other researchers had already established that nostalgia increases feelings of social support among lonely individuals. But does nostalgia help lonely people feel more socially confident and motivated?

We tested this across several studies while also confirming that loneliness is self-reinforcing. In one, we used the social-engagement task previously described in which participants were given the opportunity to select studies to participate in that would involve interacting with other people. Lonely people should want to do this, right? It would help them reduce their loneliness by giving them an opportunity to be around other people and perhaps make new connections. But this isn't what we found. Consistent with past research indicating that lonely people tend to withdraw from others, we found that people high in loneliness were less interested in the opportunity to interact with others than people who scored low in loneliness.

Importantly, nostalgia eliminated this effect. It made lonely people just as interested in an opportunity to interact with others as nonlonely people. We also found that nostalgia made lonely people more socially confident, more motivated to build friendships, and more dedicated to solving relationship problems. Nostalgia can't cure loneliness, but it can help people find the confidence and motivation they need to take steps to build or restore relationships, which is what people need to cure or gain relief from their loneliness.

If you're currently experiencing loneliness or struggling with self-doubts about your ability to repair or build relationships, nostalgia can help. Try keeping a nostalgia journal that you regularly write in, perhaps daily. Include memories that highlight social success. These should be experiences in which you had positive social interactions or that showcased your ability to make a positive difference in someone's life. This could be something as small as bringing a smile to someone's face. Next, spend several minutes writing about the experience and how it makes you feel. Try to also think about ways this experience can help you work on improving your social life today. Use these memories to take a more positive and broader perspective on your current social situation. Do these memories help you see a larger social picture? Can they remind you that your current situation is just one moment in time? Do they give you reasons to feel more optimistic about your ability to reconnect with people or build new relationships? Dig deep into your nostalgia and look for social inspiration. What can you learn from these memories to improve your social life in the present and the future?

Summary Notes for "Nostalgia Strengthens and Builds Relationships"

- Loneliness is correlated with depression, cognitive decline, compromised immunity, poor sleep, and elevated blood pressure. Chronic loneliness has even been linked to the types of cancer and cardiovascular disease that result in early death.

- We're more likely to become nostalgic when we experience negative emotions, including loneliness. Loneliness increases nostalgia, which in turn restores feelings of social support.

- Engaging in nostalgia makes us feel more optimistic about our future, including our social lives, especially when we reflect on nostalgic memories that highlight previous social achievements.

- Nostalgia fosters the type of optimism and confidence we need to form and maintain close relationships, especially when those relationships are under stress.

- Nostalgia doesn't just make us want to reconnect with friends and family; it encourages us to become more outgoing and reach out to people we don't know.

CHAPTER 8

NOSTALGIA CONNECTS YOU TO GROUPS

We're at our best when working cooperatively with others in pursuit of shared goals. Groups can consist of a handful of people (such as an office team working on a project) or they can be quite large (a city or nation). In large groups, individuals can feel connected and motivated to act in service of the group even when that group consists mainly of people they've never met. For example, some Americans feel inspired to serve their country by entering military service even though they'll only ever know a tiny percentage of their fellow citizens.

A broad group identity shared with complete strangers who are spread across a nation (and even the world) can facilitate in-person social connections and help people make new friends. For example, that person who joins the military out of a strong commitment to their national group identity will also form strong bonds with a small group of fellow soldiers.

Sometimes a broad group identity starts with a more personal social connection. Someone might become a fan of college football, for instance, because they attended a particular college or grew up nearby. Most football fans don't have a relationship with any of the team's players; they likely built their group identity as a loyal fan based on close relationships with friends or family members. Maybe they attended games with college pals, or perhaps their parents took them to games. Whatever the case, their group identity expands beyond that immediate circle of people, and it makes them feel connected with others long after they finish their degree and/or move away from the area.

Dedicated college football fans will travel long distances to attend games, especially rivalry or bowl games. Some airlines have even created flying routes specifically around such games. Sometimes fans travel to these games and meet up with old friends, and often they make new friends at activities such as tailgating parties.

You don't even have to attend a game in person to make new connections. When people wear school colors and logos, they send a clear signal to others that, at some level, they identify with a particular group. This can create opportunities to converse with strangers who are also fans. Imagine moving to a new city and seeing someone in a sports bar wearing a sweatshirt representing the college you attended. The college is far away, but this person's signaling has created an opportunity for you to introduce yourself and ask them questions. Group-identity signaling like this could even lead to a new friendship.

College football may seem like a trivial example, but it illustrates something quite powerful. Groups transcend the lives of individuals—players change and fans move away and age, but it matters little: groups are symbolic identities that typically aren't constrained by space or time. Being part of an enduring group connects people across generations. It unites us around shared goals.

In short, groups broaden our social lives. They facilitate collective activity by connecting us to people who are beyond our immediate social networks. They also foster and strengthen close-knit relationships. Nostalgia plays an important role in all of this. In fact, it's a central feature of group life.

Collective Nostalgia Versus Personal Nostalgia

So far in this book I've mostly focused on *personal nostalgia*. Personal nostalgia is autobiographical—it's rooted in experiences from our own lives and involves experiences shared with family and friends. *Collective nostalgia*, on the other hand, is a nostalgic experience in which we think of ourselves in terms of a particular social identity or as a member of a certain group, and the nostalgia concerns events or objects related to that group. Going back to the college football example, if someone is nostalgic for a time when they attended a championship game and celebrated with a bunch of other team fans, that would be an experience of collective nostalgia because the group identity played a key role in that experience. That experience also involved personal nostalgia because it included more private moments with close friends, but it's more than personal—the memory implicates a broader group identity.

Historical nostalgia can involve personal and collective nostalgia, but it doesn't have to. Imagine someone who feels nostalgic for 1980s America, something that's common among middle-aged people today. Nostalgia for that time might involve personal memories, which would make it both historical and personal. I grew up in the '80s, so I have experiences that enrich the sentimental feelings I have for the cultural products of that time. When I listen to music from that decade, it often (but not always) triggers specific memories, though I am also nostalgic for '90s music because that's when I was in high school and college.

I've interacted with adults who were born in the early 2000s but who love the 1980s. They're obsessed with the fashion, music, and movies of that period of time, which occurred decades before they started developing their own pop cultural tastes. I used to hang out at a retro arcade brewery that had a bunch of arcade games from the '80s and '90s and there were frequently customers who were in their early to midtwenties. They weren't around when those games first came out, but these people still felt nostalgic toward them. My historical nostalgia for the '80s involves personal nostalgia; theirs doesn't.

Have you ever felt nostalgic for a time when you weren't alive? Have you ever attended a costume party with a particular historical theme? Do you collect items or have hobbies that are somehow focused on a specific time in history? Do you enjoy film, music, or books about past generations?

Historical nostalgia can connect to collective nostalgia, too. One way that groups reinforce their bond across time as new members enter and old members leave is by offering a historical narrative. Going back to the example of sports, you've probably seen glass-case displays of trophies, medals, photos, and other artifacts at a high school or college. We can experience historical nostalgia in ways that don't connect us to an existing group, although it can. For instance, a collector of antique dishes may engage in this activity as a purely personal hobby that doesn't include others, or they could actively interact with other collectors. Conventions and other social events—historical reenactments, for example—bring people together who share a specific passion for the past. These gatherings illustrate how historical nostalgia can build present-day groups that engage in activities that create the content of future personal and collective nostalgia.

I like *Star Trek*, but I wouldn't say that I'm a superfan. I once attended a *Star Trek* convention more out of curiosity than anything. An actor from one of the television series was there taking questions from the audience, and it was evident that many of the fans in attendance knew a lot more about *Star Trek* than the actor who was in the show. A fan asked the actor how in a particular episode the Enterprise was able to travel in a single day to a certain world even though, based on the fan's calculations, that world would have taken much longer to reach. The actor could only respond by reminding the fan that *Star Trek* is a science-fiction series intended to entertain, not a documentary.

I also learned that people from all sorts of backgrounds and ages from all over the world are united as a group by a passion for *Star Trek*. Older fans who grew up with the original show were excited to hang out and discuss their nostalgic memories with younger fans who were only recently getting into the older shows after watching the newer shows and movies. There was a historical dimension to all of this—passing down stories about a science-fiction franchise that's been around for more than five decades. In *Star Trek* fandom—as well as fandom for all sorts of pop-culture products—personal, collective, and historical nostalgia intertwine. People share old personal and group memories as well as make new ones.

Collective Nostalgia Promotes Group Commitment and Motivation

Personal nostalgia makes us feel socially connected and socially confident. It also mobilizes our social goals. Does collective nostalgia have similar effects on group connectedness and motivation? A team of researchers led by Tim Wildschut conducted a series of studies to explore this possibility.[1]

The team first tested the proposal that reflecting on a collective nostalgic experience would increase people's positive attitudes toward their group as well as motivation to spend more time with the group. To distinguish the effects of personal nostalgia from collective nostalgia, the researchers used multiple inductions. Specifically, British undergraduate students were randomly assigned to one of four tasks: collective nostalgia, personal nostalgia, collective positive event, or no reflective task.

Participants in the collective nostalgia condition were instructed to bring to mind a nostalgic event from their student life that they'd experienced together with other students at their university. Participants in the personal nostalgic condition were instructed to think about a nostalgic event that was uniquely individual to them. In reality, collective nostalgia frequently overlaps with personal nostalgia, but the goal in this study was to make them as distinct as possible.

The students in the collective positive event condition were told to bring to mind a lucky event from their life they'd experienced with other students at their university. This condition was included to make sure any effect of the collective nostalgia condition was because of nostalgia, not just because people were having happy thoughts about a group. In the no reflective task condition, participants did not complete any type of reflection task.

After completing their reflection tasks (or no task), participants completed a questionnaire assessing their positive feelings toward the group. Specifically, they rated the extent to which students at their university were "humorous," "warm," "flexible," "fun to be with," "dependable," and "trustworthy." The researchers wanted to find out if collective nostalgia increased positive evaluations of other members of the group (in this case, other students at the university).

The research team was also interested in seeing if collective nostalgia motivates people to become more active or engaged in the group. This would suggest that collective nostalgia is more than just a passing feeling; it serves as a group motivator. The researchers had participants rate their level of agreement with items concerning the extent to which they wanted to be involved with other students (as a group) at the university, such as "I want to talk to them" and "I want to spend time with them."

Collective nostalgia uniquely affects group psychology. Participants in the collective nostalgia condition rated the group significantly more positively than participants in all other conditions. Similarly, collective nostalgia, relative to all other conditions, increased motivation to become more actively engaged with the group.

Collective nostalgia does more than make us feel good about our group identities; it mobilizes us to engage in behavior that helps these groups continue to thrive.

In another study, Tim Wildschut and his team further explored the group-motivating power of collective nostalgia.[2] When people reflect nostalgically on an experience shared with a group, they subsequently feel more positive about that group and experience a greater motivation to engage the group, but does collective nostalgia inspire the type of engagement that requires commitment and personal sacrifice? To test this, after completing one of the reflection tasks previously described, participants were provided with information about a publicity campaign the university was planning. For this campaign, the university was looking for current students to volunteer time. Participants were then asked how many hours (0–10) they'd be willing to volunteer.

Collective nostalgia, relative to all other conditions, increased the number of hours participants were willing to volunteer for the group. Collective nostalgia does more than make us feel good about our group identities; it mobilizes us to engage in behavior that helps these groups continue to thrive.

The effect of collective nostalgia on group motivation persists even when a long time has passed since the individual was actively involved with a group. Consider college alumni. Many people feel nostalgic for their university years throughout their adult lives, which is good news for university fundraising. In one study, researchers found that the more university alumni felt nostalgic for their college experience, the more they wanted to socialize with other alumni, volunteer for their university, and donate money. According to the Council for Advancement and Support of Education, alumni donated $14 billion to US colleges and universities in 2022.[3]

I've spoken to a large number of alumni donors and nearly all of them express collective nostalgia for their college experience. Their donations are often driven by a desire to pass that nostalgic experience down to future students. These donors believe that it wasn't just the education they received in college that helped make them successful but also the relationships and broader group identity they developed.

The Importance of Group Identity

Think back for a minute about the self-concept discussion. Remember, people have multiple identities, including those pertaining to groups, and these identities vary in how central they are to the self-concept. Some college students, for instance, strongly identify with their school, whereas other don't. The studies just described show that collective nostalgia can strengthen group identity, but might the strength or importance of that group identity also influence the power of collective nostalgia?

The perceived importance of a group identity may be especially relevant for groups people belong to but didn't choose. For example, most people don't pick their national identity; they're born into a given country and live there until they die. Interestingly, it's common for immigrants who become US citizens to feel more patriotic about America than people who were born here. Indeed, surveys find that immigrant American citizens are more likely to report feeling proud to be American than natural-born citizens.[4] Often their American story is more central in their lives because they moved here for the opportunity to make a better life for themselves and their families, and they feel exceptionally fortunate for the opportunity.

Of course, people born in the US can also strongly identify with being American. I conducted research examining national pride and found that most US citizens are proud to be American regardless of their political affiliation, religion, race, gender, education level, and income. However, a minority of Americans (around 13 percent) don't feel this way.[5] I suspect for them, collective nostalgia related to nationality wouldn't serve as a powerful motivator. Maybe it would inspire them to feel more sentimental toward their country, but I doubt it would make them want to engage in behavior focused on their national identity.

In general, the more people view a particular group as important to their identity, the more they are willing to serve that group and make personal sacrifices for it. This suggests that collective nostalgia will have the greatest impact on group-related motivation and behavior among those who strongly identify with that group.

Tim Wildschut's team tested this idea in a study involving Irish people.[6] First, participants reported how important their Irish identity was to them. Next, they reflected on a nostalgic event they experienced with other Irish people (collective nostalgia) or an ordinary event they'd shared with other Irish people (collective ordinary event).

Collective nostalgia inspires us to serve our group, particularly if that group is central to our identity.

The researchers wanted to do something that would give participants of the study the chance to stand up for their fellow Irish citizens. To do this, they used a computer game. Participants were led to believe that they were playing a resource distribution game online with other players and that they would be randomly assigned to a particular role in the game. In reality, all participants were assigned to the role of observer. This role involved monitoring the other players. As an observer, the participant was able to punish other participants if they didn't reasonably distribute tokens (money) to a third player. This set the stage for a group-identity task. The researchers created names for the other players that would indicate whether they were part of their group (Irish) or a member of an outgroup (from another country). The procedure was also designed such that the outgroup member did not distribute much money to the player from the participant's group (the fellow Irish individual).

The researchers were interested in the extent to which participants wanted to spend their own allocated tokens to punish the outgroup player. Collective nostalgia significantly increased the number of tokens participants sacrificed in order to punish the outgroup player who transgressed against the ingroup player. Critically, this effect was only found for participants who scored high on Irish group identification.

In other words, among people who highly identified with being Irish, collective nostalgia motivated a willingness to make a personal sacrifice for a fellow Irish individual who'd been treated unfairly. Collective nostalgia inspires us to serve our group, particularly if that group is central to our identity.

Bring to mind a collective nostalgic memory. More specifically, think about one that involves a group that's important to your identity. How does this memory make you feel about your group? Does it inspire you to engage with this group more? Can you think of a nostalgic memory involving a group that makes you want to serve that group and engage in activities that ensure the group thrives in the future?

Collective nostalgia is a powerful resource for group survival. The future success of a group might depend heavily on the extent its members have nostalgic feelings about it. This is a useful example of how nostalgia isn't a barrier to future-oriented thinking but rather a critical feature of it.

If you want a group you belong to in the present to continue long into the future, it's important to cultivate group experiences that create nostalgic memories. When a group faces challenges and an uncertain future, it needs members to come together and put their personal interests aside to serve larger goals. The more members feel a sense of collective nostalgia, the more they'll be inspired to unite and make personal sacrifices for the group.

The Potential Dark Side of Collective (and Historical) Nostalgia

We all need groups. They help us organize ourselves in pursuit of shared goals, they build a social fabric that extends beyond our families and close relationships, and they often bring joy and meaning to our lives. Combined with the advanced intellectual capacities that make humans creative and innovative organisms, the ability to form, maintain, and coordinate large groups is what makes successful communities possible. But there's also a dark side to group psychology.

The Holocaust is a powerful example of how group psychology can contribute to horrible atrocities. Six million European Jews were systematically murdered by the Nazi German regime and its allies between the mid-1930s and 1940s. Tragically, the Holocaust is not a unique tragedy. Genocides, mass murders, and other crimes against humanity are reoccurring features of history that continue to occur today. In 2021, the secretary of state of the United States released a report calling out genocide and related atrocities in six nations: Myanmar (also known as Burma), China, Ethiopia, Iraq, Syria, and South Sudan.[7]

The horrors of World War II inspired a considerable amount of theory and research in the field of social psychology. One of the most important contributions to the study of group psychology was inspired by Henri Tajfel's personal experience.[8] Tajfel was a Polish Jew living in France who volunteered to serve in the French military during World War II. He was eventually captured and spent years in different prisoner-of-war camps. Tajfel miraculously survived, but after the war he discovered that all of his immediate family and many of his friends did not. This experience motivated him to study the nature of prejudice and conflict between groups, which eventually led to the development of one of the most significant theories in social psychology: *social identity theory*.

Social identity theory proposes that we don't just define ourselves in terms of individual characteristics but that our group/social identities are critical as well. We naturally categorize everything we encounter—objects, animals, people—to efficiently make sense of the world, but categorizing people can be tricky. In general, we're inclined to favor people we see as part of our group, and this tendency creates the potential for group-related bias.

Our tendency to think about ourselves and others in terms of group membership is so powerful that we do it even when there's little reason to do so. Tajfel and his colleagues discovered this by conducting studies on what's referred to as the *minimal group paradigm*.[9] Specifically, Tajfel wanted to determine what the minimal conditions are for people to show a bias in favor of their own group at the expense of another group. Some groups have long histories of rivalries and conflict between them that lead their members to dislike and even want to harm members of the opposing group, but Tajfel learned in his studies that bias in favor of own's own group happens even when group division is extremely arbitrary.

For instance, Tajfel had British schoolboys estimate the number of dots flashed on a screen. He then randomly divided the children into two groups by informing some that they'd either underestimated or overestimated the number of dots. Clearly these are silly groups; they don't involve shared experiences or personally meaningful beliefs. But they are groups nonetheless, and this fact gave the boys a way to divide themselves from others. After these groups were created, the boys completed a task that involved allocating money to the other boys in the study. Tajfel found that the boys were more likely to give money to members of their own group than to members of the other. Keep in mind that these groups shared no history and would have no ongoing future. Participants could have distributed the money equally, but they showed a clear preference for their fellow underestimators or overestimators.

This finding and many others like it helped social psychologists to understand the nature of human social cognition (a term I talked about in the previous chapter). Simple acts of categorization pave the way for bias, prejudice, and ultimately social conflict. Give people a reason to see themselves as connected to others in a group—even an obviously superficial reason—and their minds naturally favor those group members.

Such favoritism isn't entirely bad. Group loyalty can be quite beneficial, especially when the group isn't arbitrary and is developed around specific beliefs and aspirations that aren't rooted in the desire to harm others. But there's little doubt that our tendency to view the world through the lens of ingroups and outgroups can lead to harmful social conflict. Once we start favoring those who belong to our group, it's easy to start down the path of being prejudiced against other groups. Throw in other variables—competition over scarce resources, conflicting ideologies, histories that involve suffering at the hands of members of an outgroup, and emotions such as fear and anger—and thinking about people as part of an ingroup or outgroup can lead to serious social conflicts, including war and its accompanying acts of violence.

Politicians and other leaders can (and often do) exploit collective and historical nostalgia to rally support for their campaign or cause.

If collective nostalgia promotes one's commitment to a group and motivation to serve it, might collective nostalgia also contribute to social problems related to groups? In a study conducted in the Netherlands, researchers measured collective nostalgia related to national identity by asking Dutch participants to rate their agreement with statements such as "How often do you experience nostalgia when you think about the Netherlands of the past?" and "How often do you long for the good old days of the country?"[10] Participants then rated how positively they felt about various non-Western immigrant groups in the Netherlands. The researchers found that higher national nostalgia was associated with less positive feelings toward these outgroups.

But just because national nostalgia and anti-immigrant attitudes are correlated doesn't mean national nostalgia is to blame for prejudicial feelings. That being said, such research suggests we should be concerned that certain types of collective nostalgia have the potential to lead to damaging outcomes. Sometimes collective nostalgia is more about an idealized historical period than a real experience with a group. Politicians and other leaders can (and often do) exploit collective and historical nostalgia to rally support for their campaign or cause.

When people use collective and historical nostalgia to argue that the past was superior, I encourage you to be skeptical and to ask yourself a few questions, beginning with *What specific aspects of the past were better?* and *For whom?* Maybe there were some ways the past was more favorable than the present, but it's likely an oversimplification to believe that the past was better for all parties involved. Would you trade today's advances in medicine for the treatments that were in practice fifty (or 150) years ago? Even if you think you'd be happier if society were more like it was decades ago, it doesn't mean that members of other groups would feel likewise.

Historical nostalgia isn't necessarily bad. It can help bring people together and motivate needed action. For instance, a leader who seeks to unite Americans to take on a major challenge of our time might invoke nostalgia for a time in history in which Americans as a group came together to make personal sacrifices for a common cause. In the next chapter I'll discuss how nostalgia can help people be more compassionate and helpful. Collective nostalgia can be employed to divide people along group lines, but it can also be used to help people connect with others as part of a broader group.

Summary Notes for "Nostalgia Connects You to Groups"

- Personal nostalgia involves our friends, family, and experiences from our own lives, whereas collective nostalgia is about events, ideas, or objects related to our membership in given groups.

- Historical nostalgia often involves our personal and collective experiences, but it doesn't need to.

- Membership in an enduring group connects us to others across time and space and unites us in shared ideas and goals.

- Collective nostalgia inspires feelings of belongingness, but it also encourages us to help the groups we identify with to survive and thrive.

- The more important a group is to our identity, the more willing we are to make personal sacrifices to serve that group.

- We typically favor members of our own groups, and this tendency often leads to group-related bias.

- Historical nostalgia can be employed to manipulate people, but it can also bring people together to work for the benefit of all.

CHAPTER 9

NOSTALGIA HELPS YOU CARE ABOUT OTHERS

A certain amount of self-centeredness is necessary. Who else is better positioned to speak for us, to represent our needs, preferences, concerns, and goals? If we want to live self-determined lives, we must advocate for ourselves. When we always put others first, it often means that we're neglecting our own health and well-being.

Then again, our own health and well-being can suffer if we're too self-focused. People who only look out for themselves typically don't do well socially in the long run, even if they enjoy some success in certain areas of their lives. Think of the character portrayed in countless books and films who is financially successful but lonely. To fully flourish, humans need healthy relationships, and healthy relationships require us to give as well as receive.

Caring about others is part of our nature. Evolutionary psychologists point out that we're especially inclined to help and make personal sacrifices for those who are genetically related to us. Generally speaking, we're more likely to help immediate family before extended family, and extended family before nonfamily. However, the creative nature of human psychology is such that we can develop social bonds with people who feel like family, and we're sometimes more inclined to connect with friends who share our beliefs and interests than with family members who don't. As discussed in the previous chapter, we also invest in group identities that make us feel connected to people outside of our inner social circle.

Even though nostalgia is sometimes weaponized to promote division and conflict, it is also used to improve the world. Nostalgia plays an important role in promoting prosocial behavior. It inspires us to think more about our family and friends. It pushes us to serve the groups we belong to. It makes us more charitable toward strangers in need. And it can help us empathize with those who are struggling or vulnerable in some way.

Nostalgia Activates the Prosocial Mind

In chapter 7, I detailed the social power of nostalgia. Nostalgia combats loneliness. It helps us feel connected and, critically, motivates us to connect. In other words, nostalgia helps us regulate our social needs; it orients our minds toward the social world.

Nostalgia centralizes others in our awareness.

Sure, nostalgia helps us with self-discovery and development, but it also steers us away from selfishness. Cultivating a true self is not the same thing as being overly self-focused. In fact, when people focus their attention on figuring out what is most important to the self, they become more aware of the centrality of close relationships. Self-development and social motivation go hand in hand.

Remember, most of the life experiences that populate our nostalgic memories involve loved ones. We can be nostalgic for all sorts of things (music, movies, fashions, cars, and specific time periods of our lives), but most of the time our nostalgia involves others, and this encourages prosocial thoughts, goals, and behaviors. Nostalgia centralizes others in our awareness. When our minds are focused on others, we're more likely to think about what's going on in their lives as well as our own.

A research participant in one of my studies offered a perfect example of how nostalgia focuses our thoughts on others. Her memory involved, when she was thirteen, going on a shopping trip to the Mall of America in Minneapolis with her older sister. The participant described how this was a big deal to her; she always looked up to her older sister but rarely hung out with her because her sister was nearly eight years older. But one weekend, her sister asked if she wanted to make a road trip as a girls' day out, and the two had a great time together. Critically, this participant noted that revisiting this memory helps remind her how important it is to check in with her sister more frequently, especially because the two live far apart and rarely talk.

If you would like to spend more time thinking about others, regular nostalgia exercises could help. Try keeping a nostalgia journal. Set aside five to ten minutes every day or once a week to write about a nostalgic memory that involves others. This will help you activate your prosocial mind. It might be especially helpful if you'd like to spend more time thinking about the needs of those you care about but don't regularly interact with.

Nostalgia Reduces Antisocial Responses to Social Pain

Let's revisit the issue of loneliness and other forms of social exclusion. Remember, loneliness and social exclusion can be self-reinforcing because when people feel disconnected from others, they tend to become more socially defensive. This is a way to reduce further social harm. If someone rejects or excludes you, it's tempting to avoid other social activities because they might lead to more experiences of rejection or exclusion. You can't be mistreated by others if you stay far away from them. This understandable defensive response to social disconnection leads to further disconnection and can make people less prosocial.

For instance, studies have found that when people are encouraged to view their future social lives pessimistically, they become less inclined to feel empathy for people who are suffering emotionally or physically.[1] Other research similarly finds that social exclusion reduces people's willingness to help others in need and donate to charity.[2] Studies also indicate that social exclusion increases hostility and aggression.[3] Longitudinal research—research that involves following the same group of people over time—further indicates that being socially excluded predicts future increased aggression and lower cooperation.[4] When people's social needs aren't met, they withdraw to protect themselves from further social pain and develop a more antisocial disposition.

Since nostalgia is a resource that helps combat social disconnection, it's also a way to reduce the antisocial thoughts, feelings, and behaviors that result from social disconnection. Studies find that after an experience of social exclusion, spending a few minutes writing about a source of social support (such as a family member or friend) reduces the detrimental effects of social exclusion.[5] Nostalgic memories typically involve close relationships and make people feel socially supported, so they're an excellent resource for reducing antisocial responses to disconnection and encouraging the type of prosocial responses that can help restore positive social health.

If you're currently experiencing loneliness or suffering from some form of social pain, ask yourself if it's negatively affecting how you think about people. Are you becoming more cynical and less tolerant toward others? Do you find it hard to trust others? Do you find yourself being easily annoyed by them? Have you been avoiding or hostile toward people? If so, bring to mind a nostalgic experience—ideally one that involves a rewarding social activity. It might be helpful to set aside specific times to engage in nostalgic reflection as well as activities such as journaling or scrapbooking that allow you to revisit these social experiences in a deeper way. How might these experiences be useful for changing your attitudes and actions toward others in the present?

Nostalgia Encourages Reciprocity

Reciprocity is believed to be a universal norm and one that serves an important role in societal flourishing. Healthy societies require norms that promote social trust, cooperation, and generosity. Many studies show that people are more likely to comply with a request from someone who has done something for them.[6] Even subtle acts of giving can promote reciprocity. Research has found that waitstaff who greeted their customers with a large smile received larger tips and smiles in return from their customers than waitstaff who met customers with a minimal smile.[7]

For the people we regularly interact with, reciprocity is often abstract. We do something to help them because we believe that they would do the same for us. We typically don't monitor the exchange closely or expect anything in return immediately; we simply follow a reciprocity worldview when it comes to close relationships.

But if a stranger does something kind for us anonymously, we feel more inclined to pay it forward. You've probably seen a news story about a pay-it-forward chain (such as a person paying someone else's bill at a restaurant) that then motivates the first beneficiary in the chain to do the same for another customer. In 2020, a Dairy Queen in Brainard, Minnesota, experienced a chain like this that lasted for nearly three days.[8]

Nostalgia can inspire this sort of reciprocity, too. Since nostalgia makes us feel socially connected, it gets us thinking about other people and reminds us how our relationships with them benefit us. When we think about what others do for us, we become more motivated to do things for them.

In families, reciprocity can resemble the pay-it-forward phenomenon by recreating cherished experiences from one's own childhood. In one of my studies, a research participant wrote about how her memories of family picnics as a child inspired her to keep the tradition going with her husband and children. On summer weekends, her mom and dad would pack a bunch of food and games and take her and her siblings to a nearby state park for the afternoon. She remembered her dad being quite busy running a business, and these family picnics were special times together in which he wasn't distracted with work. She was a busy professional and mother herself, so revisiting those memories made her feel a duty to reciprocate by giving her children similar experiences.

Earlier in this chapter, I suggested keeping a nostalgia journal to help get you thinking about the needs of others. To enhance this activity, specifically note aspects of nostalgic memories that involve acts of kindness from others.

The Prosocial Power of Gratitude

Gratitude plays a central role in people's desire to reciprocate and help others. In my work, I find that feelings of gratitude are a common feature of nostalgia narratives. In one of my studies that focused on nostalgia among older adults, a research participant wrote about a memory involving her late husband, who died the year before. The memory was about a trip they took together to Italy. As long as she could remember, Italy was at the top of her list of places to visit. She and her husband didn't have a lot of money, and overseas travel seemed excessive, especially to her fiscally conservative husband. But he knew she wanted to visit Italy, so he promised he'd take her. After they raised their kids and saved money for the trip, they were able to make it happen. This participant didn't write much about the actual trip. In fact, she noted that although she enjoyed seeing Italy, what made this memory special to her was that it was an example of how much her late husband loved her and wanted to make her happy. An international vacation is not something he would've chosen on his own. She closed her narrative by describing how grateful this memory made her feel. She missed her husband and had been struggling with profound sadness since his passing, but memories like the one she wrote about helped her deal with the loss because they reminded her of how blessed her life had been.

Many studies find that feelings of gratitude promote positive mental and physical health. Research involving daily or weekly gratitude writing exercises has found that gratitude increases a range of positive mental states—greater optimism, happiness, and feelings of belongingness—in addition to physical health-related behaviors.[9] Gratitude doesn't just make people feel good; it motivates action. In other research, participants with an anxiety or depression diagnosis reported lower levels of depression and stress and greater well-being after engaging in gratitude-focused diary writing for three weeks.[10]

In your nostalgia journaling, list the ways in which nostalgic experiences make you feel grateful.

Gratitude also makes people more prosocial. Studies show that when people feel grateful, they're more likely to pay attention to the ways their romantic partner supports them. They are also more empathetic toward others. Gratitude also makes people less aggressive, likely because it promotes empathy. Studies also find that gratitude increases the amount of money people give to charity.[11]

Nostalgia Inspires You to Help Strangers

Perhaps one of our greatest strengths as humans (or at least one of our most redeeming ones) is our willingness to help strangers. Throughout history, people have made great sacrifices, even willingly giving their lives, to help people they've never met. Though our daily news is dominated with stories about the problems of the world, every day there are people from different walks of life all around the world who devote themselves to helping others, including strangers.

The prosocial motivational power of nostalgia starts with family and friends and extends beyond them to the groups we belong to and the communities we live in. This makes sense because a lot of our nostalgic memories involve loved ones and people we regularly interact with as part of the groups we're affiliated with or those who reside in our local community. But nostalgia also has the potential to inspire us to help strangers.

In a study conducted by Xinyue Zhou and her colleagues, undergraduate Chinese students brought to mind a nostalgic or ordinary experience and then wrote down four keywords related to the experience.[12] The researchers then presented the participants with a one-page description of a fictitious nonprofit organization that existed to help young victims of a recent major earthquake. After reading the description of the charity, participants were instructed to write down the number of hours and amount of money they'd be willing to donate to this charity. As you might expect, participants in the nostalgia condition reported a greater willingness to donate time and money than those in the control condition. In another study, the researchers found the same results when they used a different fictitious charity (to show the effect wasn't specific to one cause) and a broader sample of people ranging in age from sixteen to sixty-two and representing a range of nationalities.[13]

Nostalgia inspires people to want to help others in need, but do they actually act on this desire? In a final study, the same researchers wanted to determine if they could use what they'd learned from the previous studies to create an appeal that would persuade people to engage in charitable behavior.[14] They created two versions of a charity appeal to be distributed to participants. Both versions contained information and pictures about a charity to help young earthquake victims. In one condition, the appeal contained wording intended to make people feel nostalgic ("Those Were the Days: Restoring the Past for the Children in Wenchaun"). In the control condition, the charity appeal didn't make reference to the past ("Now Is the Time: Build the Future for Children in Wenchaun").

The experiment involved Chinese college students completing a number of unrelated laboratory tasks that provided a reason for the researchers to compensate them financially. When participants thought the study was over, and they were paid, the real experiment began. As participants left the laboratory, they encountered a research assistant who handed them either the nostalgia-oriented or control (non-nostalgic) flyer for the charity. There was also a collection box in the room to allow participants to make a donation. Participants who received the nostalgia-based charity flyer donated significantly more money than participants who received the non-nostalgia flyer.

> If you're involved in charitable organizations or are planning activities to raise money for a prosocial cause, you can use nostalgia and gratitude to encourage others to give. When designing promotional materials for the cause, think about ways to introduce a nostalgia theme. You could also ask potential donors to share a nostalgic experience in which they benefited in some way from others. Then ask them to share how this makes them feel. I suspect gratitude will be one of the emotions they express.

Other research indicates that nostalgia more broadly makes people helpful. For example, my colleagues and I created an experiment that gave participants an opportunity to help someone.[15] To begin, the research participants completed a nostalgia or ordinary autobiographical writing task. Following that, a research assistant entered the laboratory room carrying a box of pencils and a folder of papers. In what appeared to be an accident, the researcher spilled the box of pencils on the floor. Participants in the nostalgia condition were more likely to help the experimenter pick up the pencils than participants in the control condition. Once more, we found that nostalgia energizes prosocial action.

Nostalgia Makes You More Likely to Seek Help

My colleague Jacob Juhl at the University of Southampton, along with a team of researchers in the UK and China, also discovered that nostalgia makes people more likely to ask for help.[16] Juhl's team conducted many studies exploring the link between nostalgia and help-seeking, and all of the studies showed that when people feel nostalgic, they were more willing and more likely to ask others for help.

In one study, after spending a few minutes thinking and writing about a nostalgic experience or thinking and writing about a non-nostalgic experience, research participants were presented with a puzzle task. What they didn't realize was that the puzzle was unsolvable. The researchers were interested in how long it would take for people to ask for help. After setting up the task for participants, the research assistant informed them that if they wanted help solving the problem, they just needed to press a button on the intercom system in the room and someone would come help. The researchers recorded how long it took participants to request help. They found that participants in the nostalgia condition took a significantly shorter amount of time than those in the control condition. This finding converged with other studies they conducted that showed that participants in a nostalgic condition reported feeling more comfortable asking others for help than participants in a control condition.[17]

Nostalgia makes us more humane.

The most obvious benefit of asking for help is receiving it. Regardless of how independent and self-sufficient we imagine ourselves to be, the fact is that we need others to thrive. But there are other, broader prosocial benefits to requesting assistance from others. Being willing to ask for help when we need it gives others the opportunity to be generous, which further promotes reciprocity, gratitude, and the general spirit of giving.

It's important that people feel needed and know that others benefit from their assistance. When people are both offering help to others and asking for help when they need it, they're building and sustaining the types of cooperative and collaborative relationships and communities that lead to individual and societal flourishing. That nostalgia contributes to both sides of prosocial behavior—seeking and giving—further indicates that it plays a vital role in human social life.

The many ways that nostalgia promotes sociality and prosocial behaviors speak to a broader point: nostalgia makes us more humane. It helps us feel connected to family, friends, and the groups we belong to. It motivates us to focus on those connections and strengthen them. It encourages us to empathize and help others, even those we've never met and never will. And it pushes us to ask others for help when we need it.

Summary Notes for "Nostalgia Helps You Care about Others"

- Nostalgia inspires us to think more about our loved ones, serve the groups we belong to, and act more charitably to strangers in need.

- Nostalgia reduces the detrimental thoughts, feelings, and behaviors that accompany social disconnection.

- Nostalgia inspires reciprocity. It encourages us to reflect on relationships and foster a sense of mutual benefit.

- Not only does nostalgia make us more generous and helpful but it also motivates us to ask for help when we need it.

PART 4

HOW NOSTALGIA MAKES LIFE MEANINGFUL

CHAPTER 10

NOSTALGIA HELPS YOU COPE WITH EXISTENTIAL FEARS

We are all going to die someday. This isn't a pleasant observation or an especially uplifting way to start a chapter, but it's a fact. And it's a fact that humans seem to be uniquely aware of.

In his 1973 book *The Denial of Death*, which won the Pulitzer Prize in 1974, the cultural anthropologist Ernest Becker articulated this distinctly existential dilemma. On the one hand, like other organisms, we're in the survival game, which means we're oriented toward avoiding death. Unlike other organisms, however, we humans are burdened with the knowledge of our inevitable demise. We know that regardless of how much we exercise, maintain a healthy diet, avoid dangerous activities, and keep up with all our recommended health screenings, eventually our physical bodies will succumb to mortality.

According to Becker and other existential scholars, this conflict between our instinct for life and our awareness of unavoidable death has the potential to cause a great deal of anxiety.[1] And yet with the exception of a small percentage of people suffering from severe mental illness, people all over the world get up every day and live relatively healthy lives, psychologically speaking. We don't hide in our homes paralyzed about the dangers of the world. We don't approach each birthday debilitated with the existential dread of knowing that we're one year closer to the end of our lives. Instead, we continue to fulfill our duties and pursue our goals and interests. We even fearlessly do things that we know can endanger or shorten our lives. We experience the normal ups and downs that are part of life—pleasure and pain, success and loss, and triumph and tragedy—but surprisingly few of us live in constant fear of death, despite the fact that we know it's certain.

Becker argued that the reason humans aren't overwhelmed by existential terror from the awareness of death is because we invest in cultural belief systems or worldviews that provide enduring meaning or self-transcendence. Religion often provides a direct answer to the problem of death by offering a dualist (body and spirit) framework for people to think about the self. The body dies but the spirit lives on in an afterlife, via reincarnation, or in some other form of spiritual existence.

Becker and other scholars also argued that humans don't have to believe in literal immortality to solve the problem of death. We can symbolically mitigate the threat of death awareness by investing in social and cultural identities that transcend the mortal limits of the physical self. For instance, our families allow us to gain existential comfort by thinking about the continuation of our genetic line. Contributions to society allow us to leave an impact on the world after we're gone. This is the power of legacy. Collective identities (such as being part of a group that existed well before us and likely will exist long into the future) also help us define the self as larger and more enduring than our individual mortality would allow.

This is one reason people become offended when their cherished cultural symbols are defiled. To someone who highly identifies with their nationality, for example, burning the nation's flag isn't just an act of material destruction; it's an attack on a transcendent identity.

Culture is key to all these sources of existential comfort. It provides a framework for the narratives we use to respond to existential questions and fears about death and related topics. Culture helps us craft a self-concept that's fortified against existential terror as well as a self-concept that has enduring meaning.

Nostalgia plays a vital role in this battle against existential anxiety. Think about the memories you cherish most. Consider how many of them are embedded within cultural traditions or rites of passage. Weddings, graduations, holidays, religious rituals and ceremonies, sporting events, concerts, and vacations all take place within a cultural context. Even the most personal nostalgic memory is connected to a broader cultural framework that helps us feel transcendent in the face of unavoidable mortality.

To understand how nostalgia and culture work together to help us avoid existential anxiety, it's crucial to first understand how we develop a relationship with culture for the purpose of answering questions about our mortality.

Nostalgia and Existential Childhood Development

Death awareness is part of normal human development. Very young children have trouble understanding death; they tend to think it's reversible or that it doesn't affect them. But as children approach school age (between four and seven), they begin to understand the physical finality of death and that they themselves are mortal. This developmental process often involves difficult conversations following the death of a favorite pet or grandparent, or the recognition that their parents are aging and people who get old will eventually die. Over time they realize that they are on the path to death as well. This often triggers both curiosity and concern about the implications of mortality: *Do we have to die? Why? How long do people live? What is death like? Will it hurt? Will I be scared? Why do some people die young? What happens after we die?* And so on.

Some children are more bothered by the awareness of death than others. But because humans are ultimately survival-oriented, it's absolutely healthy that nearly all of us experience some fear of death in childhood before we must navigate a world without a lot of adult supervision. A child (or adult) without any concern about mortality is a tragic accident waiting to happen. Too much fear, however, is an obvious barrier to a happy and productive life. Therefore, humans need ways to engage the world without being immobilized by existential fear.

When children first become anxious about their mortality, they turn to their parents and other caregivers for answers and support. In addition to the normal social support that adults offer when children are upset, they also comfort kids by teaching them the cultural worldviews that offer existential security. These include both religious and secular worldviews.

As kids become teenagers and young adults, they begin to develop their own ways of thinking about the world and its mysteries. Often they're heavily influenced by their families and broader social environment they live in, but individual agency and self-development also play important roles. This means emerging adults must decide what cultural beliefs and traditions from their upbringing they want to carry forward as well as what new ones they want to explore and adopt. When adults grapple with existential concerns about mortality, they need the cultural worldviews they've adopted in order to maintain psychological well-being. They also need the motivation to take the types of risks that are necessary for them and society to thrive.

Nostalgia plays a vital role here. The more nostalgic adults feel about past experiences connected to the cultural worldviews their parents taught them, the more likely they are to want to continue those beliefs and traditions. Just like alumni are more likely to donate money to the college they attended if they have nostalgic memories of their time in college, we are more likely to invest in cultural beliefs and practices if we have nostalgic memories about them.

Using the Past to Fight the Future

When I first started studying nostalgia, I was more interested in the human ability to think about the future and how this might both inspire and frighten us. The scholars I was working with at the time had spent a couple of decades turning Ernest Becker's ideas into testable hypotheses. They wanted to see if what Becker proposed about death awareness was true. Do people use cultural worldviews and related group identities as ways to prevent existential anxiety about death?

In their studies, these scholars observed that having people spend a few minutes thinking about their mortality increased their desire to have children, their commitment to romantic partners, their degree of patriotism, and their level of religious faith.[2] This was especially likely for beliefs and identities that were already important to the participants' sense of self. For instance, thinking about death is most likely to increase commitment to religious faith if one is already a person of faith. Thinking about death may generally make us more open to lots of ideas that can help us find ways to feel transcendent, but we're more likely to turn to the specific ideas we're already invested in.

In other words, when our thoughts drift toward the reality of inevitable death, we comfort ourselves by turning to the social and cultural structures that help us feel like we are more than physical organisms that are annihilated by death. Our solution to the problem of death is to seek transcendent meaning—to identify with and invest in identities that will outlive us.

When I became involved in research examining how people respond to their awareness of mortality, I started thinking specifically about the time-travel aspects of existential psychology. Being aware of mortality requires an ability to mentally time travel to the future. I started to wonder if the same ability is also used to help combat existential anxiety. When people think about their future mortality, do they turn to the past for comfort?

I thought this was a reasonable possibility because the past is full of culturally significant life experiences to reassure us that we're part of something larger and more enduring than our mortal lives. Nostalgia might serve as a critical resource for building an existential identity that offers self-transcendence.

To test this, my colleagues and I conducted studies comparing people who regularly engage in nostalgia to those who do not.[3] We hypothesized that if nostalgia helps protect people from existential anxiety, those who regularly engage in it would be less susceptible to the negative psychological effects of thinking about death. Across several studies, we found support for this idea. In one study, we had research participants complete a questionnaire about how often they reflect on nostalgic memories. We then had half of them spend a few minutes thinking and writing about their mortality, whereas the other half wrote about a topic not related to death. Finally, we administered an anxiety questionnaire. Participants who thought and wrote about death felt more anxious than those who thought and wrote about something else. Thinking about one's mortality causes anxiety, at least temporarily. However, we only found this effect among participants who reported that they didn't regularly engage in nostalgia. People who frequently reflect nostalgically on the past are less bothered by thinking about their future death.

People who frequently engage in nostalgia are less anxious about death and better able to maintain a sense of meaning in life.

We've found similar patterns when looking at other indicators of well-being. For instance, thinking about death decreases perceptions of meaning in life, but again, we only found this to be the case among those who didn't regularly engage in nostalgia.

How do we know that people who report regularly reflecting on nostalgic memories are using those memories to respond to concerns about death? In another study, we randomly assigned some people to think about death and others to think about a different topic.[4] We then gave everyone a questionnaire measuring how nostalgic they were currently feeling. We found that those who were asked to think about death became more nostalgic than those who weren't. Additionally, it was the people who reported that they regularly engaged in nostalgia that were most likely to feel nostalgic after thinking about death. People who frequently engage in nostalgia are less anxious about death and better able to maintain a sense of meaning in life when thinking about the existential threat of death.

When we face situations that remind us that life is uncertain and finite, we gain comfort from turning to the past and revisiting the memories that remind us that we are connected to families and other groups that were here before we were born and will be here long after we're gone. Nostalgia helps situate us within an enduring cultural narrative.

As previously noted, most people don't live their lives in constant existential terror. We have too much to do. We're driven by needs and goals and, critically, we have culturally influenced beliefs and identities that offer us ways to be part of something larger and longer lasting than our brief mortal lives. This helps insulate us from existential anxiety. That being said, from time to time, we come face to face with reminders of just how small, uncertain, and fragile our lives are, and this is when we're most in need of existential comfort.

If you find yourself distressed or depressed about major existential issues (such as mortality), try using nostalgia to connect with the life experiences that have made you feel transcendent. In your past, you might find the fortitude needed to approach the future with gratitude and hope, not fear.

Nostalgia Can Help You Cope with Loss

The fact that those we love are also mortal is another source of existential anxiety and sadness. Just as we want to feel like we are part of something more enduring than our brief lives, we want to feel the same about our loved ones. We're motivated to keep them alive in some way, to honor their legacy and even to maintain a connection to them after they're gone.

It's common for people to continue talking to family members after they've died and to even experience hallucinations of them. A study of widowed people found that around half of them experienced visions of their deceased spouse, especially within the first ten years of widowhood.[5] The longer they were married, the more likely the visions were. Other research finds that most widowed people who have hallucinations of deceased loved ones find these experiences pleasant and helpful.[6] Our brains are wired for social connection. Even after our loved ones die, our need to connect with them lives on.

Nostalgia is one way to stay connected to those we've lost and to make sure that they're not forgotten. If you've ever attended a funeral, you have probably experienced the way nostalgia is used by family and friends to cope with loss in the immediate aftermath of the death. As a way to celebrate someone's life and affirm our relationship with them, we share nostalgic stories. We laugh. We cry. We remember.

In the nostalgic narratives I've collected over the years, I've seen many references to memories involving loved ones who have passed. These represent some of the most bittersweet elements of nostalgia. They also reveal how nostalgia helps people cope with loss.

For example, one woman wrote about experiences from early childhood of her mother reading books to her. This was a nightly activity and one she didn't want to stop even when she was old enough to read to herself, because she loved her mother's voice and the special time just the two of them spent together. She described such memories as especially important because her mother died from cancer when quite young, and so these were some of the last memories the woman had of her. Memories like these certainly have sad elements. They made this woman miss her mother. But she also indicated that she found it important to regularly reflect on these memories because that was how she kept her mother alive in her heart. Nostalgia helped her maintain a spiritual connection—one that couldn't be severed by physical death.

Interestingly, recent research finds that spirituality and nostalgia are highly correlated.[7] People who think of themselves as highly spiritual also tend to frequently engage in nostalgia. It's worth noting that spirituality is highly social. When people describe spiritual experiences, they often mention a feeling of connectedness to others. In this way, just as nostalgia orients our minds toward the social world, it might also facilitate or support spiritual practices and experiences that offer a sense of transcendent social connection.

Nostalgic memories involving loved ones we've lost also inspire us to take actions that allow the deceased to continue to positively impact the world. People start charitable organizations to honor the memory of loved ones, for example; or they take up projects that the deceased was unable to finish, thereby allowing that person's work to continue long after death.

If you have lost loved ones and are looking for ways to honor their memory and maintain a transcendent connection with them, nostalgia can be of great value. Dive deeply into memories involving those people that might help reveal something that was both important to them and your connection with them. Were there personal causes, hobbies, or projects you shared? How can you continue to pursue those interests in a way that will not only remind you of those relationships but also bring joy or help others in some way?

Nostalgia Can Help You Avoid Existential Regrets

Nostalgia connects us to the transcendence-affirming experiences we've accumulated over our lifetime. But there is another way that nostalgia can help us in our existential battle with mortality. Nostalgia doesn't just reveal the types of goals and activities that make us feel more than mortal. It also helps us avoid wasting time on the ones that don't.

Research indicates that the most common regrets people have involve romantic relationships and family.[8] Some regrets we can do something about in the future. For example, if we wish we'd spent more time with family and friends, it might not be too late to prioritize those relationships. In fact, as we get older, it's common for us to shift our priorities away from more personal ambitions and interests and toward reconnection with loved ones.

Regrets become more existential when it's too late. You can only do so much about regretting not spending more time with a family member who is no longer alive. However, since nostalgia helps us focus on the aspects of our lives that we find most important to our self-concepts and orients us toward relationships, it can help us reduce the number of existential regrets we might experience. The more we engage in nostalgic reflection, the more we bring to mind the types of experiences we should pursue to avoid a life full of regrets.

Write down three of your most cherished nostalgic memories. What makes them so special to you? How might these memories help you create goals or plans for a more intentional life? Try using these nostalgic memories to identify at least one specific goal you can take on right now. The future is uncertain and regret is unavoidable, but you can use the memories you most cherish to live life to its fullest.

Nostalgia as a Fountain of Youth

Many adults have nostalgic memories of attending summer camp as a child. Camp is where they made new friends and reconnected with ones they only got to see at camp. It's also where they engaged in all sorts of activities that rarely happened elsewhere: canoeing, horseback riding, archery, and singing songs around a campfire, for example.

In 2021, the *Chicago Tribune* published an article titled "The Six Most Amazing Adult Summer Camps in the US." Oprah Daily published a similar article: "The Best Adult Summer Camps That Throwback to Your Childhood." I'm not personally interested in returning to summer camp, but I do have some great memories of riding motorbikes and horses and taking early-morning swims in a freezing spring-fed pool. But regardless of what aspect of our childhood and youth we long to revisit, nostalgia can help us feel young again.

Throughout history, people have embarked on all sorts of quests to recapture their youth. Notably, the sixteenth-century Spanish explorer Juan Ponce de Leon was said to have searched for magical waters that healed sickness and restored youthfulness, popularly referred to as the Fountain of Youth. The spirit of that search persists today. It can be observed in bestselling books and magazine articles offering ways for people to feel and look younger. Though we often think about efforts to restore youthfulness as being motivated by vanity, there are good reasons to strive to feel young. For example, feeling younger than one's chronological age is associated with psychological well-being and more positive attitudes about aging.[9] A youthful mindset inspires youthful optimism.

The benefits of feeling youthful extend to actual physical health. Research has found that among patients recovering from cancer, feeling younger than one's chronological age is associated with better recovery.[10] Studies have also found that even after accounting for health risk factors like smoking and body mass index, feeling younger is associated with lower levels of C-reactive protein, a marker of systemic inflammation that's been linked to increased risk for disease.[11] Feeling younger than one's chronological age is also associated with a reduced risk for death due to worsening health.[12]

Experimental research has provided causal evidence for the impact of feeling young on health-related outcomes. Specifically, researchers have found that making older adults feel younger by giving them positive feedback about their performance on a physical task caused them to outperform older adults who were given no feedback on subsequent tests of strength.[13]

Since nostalgia involves revisiting cherished memories from the past, my colleagues and I wondered if nostalgia is a resource that people use to feel younger as they age. Indeed, it's common for people to feel especially nostalgic for experiences from their childhood and teenage years. In our studies, we recruited research participants as young as eighteen and as old as seventy-two. We randomly assigned these participants to either a nostalgia or non-nostalgia control condition. In one study, we used music to induce nostalgia.[14] After all, music is a big part of people's youth. We thought that music would be especially likely to make people feel young again. Participants in the nostalgia condition were asked to conduct a YouTube search for a song that made them feel nostalgic. After finding a song, they were instructed to listen to it. Participants in the control group were asked to search for a song that they liked but only recently discovered. We did this so that both groups were listening to pleasant music but that only the nostalgia group was listening to music that connected them to their past.

After this, all participants were asked if they felt younger than their current age, about their current age, or older than their current age. As we predicted, people in the nostalgia condition were more likely to feel younger than their current age than people in the control condition. Interestingly, we also found that this pattern was only statistically significant for those forty-two years of age and older.

In a second study, we found a similar pattern using a different method for inducing nostalgia.[15] We had some participants write about a nostalgic memory, and we had others do the same about an ordinary memory. Again, we found that nostalgia made people feel younger than their actual age, but this pattern only emerged for people over the age of thirty-eight.

In yet another study, we had both those in our nostalgia condition and those in a control condition reflect on a memory from the same time point in their lives.[16] Specifically, we asked them to write about a memory from high school. Half were told this should be a nostalgic memory, and half were told this should be an ordinary memory about high school. This allowed us to better ensure that people in our nostalgia and control conditions were thinking about similar times in their lives.

Nostalgia doesn't make us younger, but it does help us maintain feelings of youthfulness as we get older.

We were also interested in looking at other indicators of a youthful mindset, so after completing the nostalgia or control writing task, we asked participants questions about their confidence in their physical abilities. Specifically, we asked them how confident they were that they could: "Do anything an average twenty-year-old of your sex can," "Lift as much as an average twenty-year-old of your sex can," "Keep up with an average twenty-year-old of your sex," "Run as long as an average twenty-year-old of your sex can," "Run as far as an average twenty-year-old of your sex can," "Jump as high as an average twenty-year-old of your sex can," and "Do as much physical activity as a twenty-year-old can do without getting overly fatigued or sore."

We then asked the participants how optimistic or pessimistic they were about their future health, the idea being that if nostalgia makes people feel young, it should also make them more confident about their physical abilities and more optimistic about their health.

Consistent with our previous findings, middle- and older-aged adults who reflected on a nostalgic experience from high school felt younger, more confident in their physical abilities, and more optimistic about their health than middle- and older-aged adults who reflected on an ordinary high school memory. Remember, both groups mentally time traveled to a similar time in their lives. But only those who accessed a nostalgic memory experienced a psychological "fountain of youth."

Together, these studies indicate that nostalgia performs this function once we head into middle age. Nostalgia doesn't make us younger, but it does help us maintain feelings of youthfulness as we get older.

As we age, it's easy to start losing our youthful spirit, to feel like we're too old for certain activities. Sometimes this is true. Physical aging is a reality. As someone who enjoys weightlifting and other physical exercises, I've learned this the hard way by sometimes not listening to my body and suffering injuries as a result—injuries that now take much longer to recover from. But there are lots of ways to modify activities and stay engaged with the physical, social, and intellectual activities that help keep us young at heart.

If you find yourself increasingly adopting an "I'm too old for that" mindset, try some nostalgia exercises. Listen to your favorite music from your youth. Watch old movies. Try some nostalgia writing activities. Dig out those old photo albums or yearbooks. Try to find a way to reconnect with the younger you. We can't go back and relive the years of our youth—and most of us don't want to. But we can use nostalgia to find some youthful energy.

Youthful energy can help us break out of our comfort zone and try new things, which further helps us take advantage of the benefits of youth. As we age, it's easy to become set in our ways. We settle into routines that give our lives structure. Structure and order are helpful, and the opposite can cause undue stress and anxiety. Once we figure out what we want out of life, what our priorities and goals are, we're especially motivated to avoid such stress and anxiety. But we also benefit from occasionally breaking up our routines to try different approaches. Introducing some spontaneity into our lives can be refreshing. It can energize new goals and spawn creative solutions to problems.

In other words, it might seem like nostalgia for our youth is a retreat from new ideas. In reality, nostalgia can reconnect us to the carefree, bold, and open-minded ways of thinking that we tend to move away from as we age.

Summary Notes for "Nostalgia Helps You Cope with Existential Fears"

- We aren't overwhelmed with the fear of death because we have cultural beliefs and worldviews that give us meaning and a sense of transcendence.

- Regularly engaging in nostalgia also protects us from existential anxiety.

- Nostalgia makes us prosocial and supports spiritual practices that provide a sense of transcendent social connection.

- Nostalgic reflection also grounds us in the types of experiences that ensure we don't live a life marked with regret.

- Middle-aged and older adults who reflect on nostalgic experiences feel younger, are more confident in their physical abilities, and are more optimistic about their health.

CHAPTER 11

NOSTALGIA FOCUSES YOU ON WHAT GIVES YOU MEANING

Much of what I've discussed in this book so far connects to the fundamental human need for meaning in life. And because we require other people to survive and thrive, much of our time is spent seeking and maintaining social connections. To this end, superficial relationships won't cut it. We require meaningful connections—bonds that make us feel needed or significant. To understand this, try the following thought exercise:

Imagine that you're incredibly wealthy and that you can easily meet your survival needs by paying others for goods and services. You never need to ask anyone for a favor or develop the type of relationships in which people do things for each other because they care deeply about each other. You can always hire professionals for advice, for help around the house, to learn new things, and so on. You can even get people to hang out with you by throwing lavish parties or always picking up the bill when you're out on the town. In this reality, you'd never be socially isolated. You'd enjoy stimulating conversations with your guitar teacher, fitness trainer, financial advisor, personal chef, and the acquaintances happy to enjoy a night out on your dime. But if none of these people were real friends—the kind of people who would still want to spend time with you even if you lost your fortune—would you call any of these meaningful relationships? I don't think so.

The reason seems obvious, but it's worth emphasizing. To be socially healthy, we need relationships that aren't based on things like wealth, beauty, or fame. Our lives aren't merely transactional—we need to feel like we matter, like we're significant contributors to a meaningful social and cultural drama. We're energized by the goals we perceive as allowing us to improve our lives and the lives of others. Humans are much more than social organisms. We're an existential species driven by a need to perceive the social aspects of life as meaningful. Ultimately our social needs implicate the quest for meaning, the quest to matter.

Nostalgia plays a crucial role in this. Not only does it help us face existential threats (the realization that we and all those we love will one day die, for example, or that tragedy can strike at any time with little or no warning); nostalgia more broadly helps us create meaning in our everyday lives. It acts as a guide, focusing our attention on where to find meaning and reminding us that in times in which meaning seems out of reach, it isn't. Without nostalgia, the quest for meaning would be difficult and probably impossible. We rely on our cherished memories to show us a way forward, particularly when the way is uncertain.

The Importance of Meaning in Life

Before digging into how nostalgia supports meaning, it's important to emphasize just how critical meaning in life is. The search for meaning isn't just an intellectual exercise for theologians, philosophers, and anyone else who likes to ponder the big questions about the nature of existence. It's a fundamental feature of the human condition. All of us are meaning-makers.

The more people feel like they're able to find meaning in life, the happier they are.

But what exactly is meaning? At a basic level, meaning-making is about making sense of the world. Humans aren't alone in this endeavor. Even my dog does this. She learns patterns and rules to accomplish her goals—for example, she knows she needs to sit at her food bowl to receive a meal. But as discussed throughout this book, humans are cognitively advanced organisms, and our high level of self-awareness means that we're not only trying to make sense of the world around us in order to navigate it but that we also turn inward to make sense of our own existence. Why are we here? What do we need to do to make life worthwhile? Can we find meaning that transcends our brief time on this planet?

Ultimately meaning is feeling that we are significant contributors to a larger picture, socially and culturally. When we feel a strong sense of meaning, we believe we're doing important things that make a difference in the world. This effort to feel personally meaningful has consequences for our mental and physical health—the more people feel like they're able to find meaning in life, the happier they are. Meaning inspires a positive and hopeful attitude. It's a vital part of our overall well-being.

A lack of meaning leads to poor mental health. When people don't perceive their lives as meaningful, they're at greater risk of depression, anxiety, and drug and alcohol abuse. Feeling meaningless is also a strong predictor of suicide. Meaninglessness puts people on a path to self-destruction.

However, when people perceive their lives as full of meaning, not only are they at less risk of suffering from mental illness and self-destructive behavior but they're also more likely to positively respond to mental health treatment if they need it. Meaning is a critical component of recovery. Regardless of how talented therapists are, they will have little success helping clients heal if those clients struggle to see life as meaningful. Even the most psychologically healthy people experience tragedies and traumas that can make them vulnerable to depression and other mental health problems. Meaning in life helps them find their way back to positive mental health.

Meaning plays a central role in mental health treatment because people who view their lives as meaningful are most likely to be motivated to recover and to comply with the treatment they receive. Meaning makes people want to get better when they are mentally suffering. It makes them more optimistic that they can get better, which further motivates them to work at improving their mental health.

The benefits of meaning extend beyond mental health. When people view their lives as full of meaning, they're more inclined to adopt and maintain healthy lifestyles. For example, people

Meaning is existential energy. who are focused on meaning are more likely to engage in physical exercise and to do so more vigorously. And just as people who have a strong sense of meaning are better able to recover from mental illness, they're also better able to recover from physical illness.[1] All of this helps explain why people who perceive their lives as meaningful tend to live longer than those who don't.

Additionally, meaning supports social health. People are more empathetic, generous, and motivated to connect with others when they feel meaningful. When people feel like they're leading meaningful lives, they're more socially energized and engaged. Meaning inspires us to connect and share with others. When we view our lives as full of meaning, we're most driven to improve our lives and the lives of others. People who lack meaning tend to be passive and lethargic, whereas people who have meaning are active and engaged. In this sense, meaning is existential energy.

What Makes Life Meaningful?

There are many paths to meaning. People have distinct personalities, opinions, interests, and goals. Think about a career that you believe would make you miserable. Undoubtedly there are people out there who'd find the same occupation extremely fulfilling. I have several family members who are in the nursing field. As someone who's easily disgusted by bodily fluids and human creatureliness more broadly, I know I'd make a horrible nurse, and yet there are millions of people in nursing and related health-care careers who feel a calling to the profession.

Of course, jobs aren't the only way to feel meaningful. What matters when it comes to meaning is that people feel valued; that they are making an important contribution to their families, communities, and broader society. This explains why some people struggle when they retire, because they never cultivated sources of meaning outside of their careers. The key to a successful retirement is to find ways to feel valued outside of work. Many retirees volunteer, in part, for this reason. They enjoy serving others in a way that makes them feel valued without needing to worry about all the constraints and demands they had to deal with during their paid employment years.

Regardless of the line of work they're in, people are most likely to perceive their careers as meaningful if they think about their jobs as serving an important societal function. Whether you're a nurse, accountant, engineer, cook, musician, plumber, farmer, entrepreneur, bus driver, writer, police officer, yoga instructor, or janitor, you're more likely to extract meaning from work if you feel like it improves the lives of others in some way.

In the early part of the COVID-19 pandemic, I watched an interview on the nightly news with a bus driver about how the pandemic had impacted his job. The reporter asked him if he was afraid of catching COVID-19 since he was driving around a bus full of strangers. The driver said he was a little bit concerned but that he also felt energized and more meaningful than ever because it became clear that he was an essential worker helping make sure some of the most vulnerable people, such as the elderly, had a way to get where they needed to go, including to medical appointments and to get tested for COVID. While many people stayed home as much as possible and attempted to avoid contact with others, this man continued to do a job that served the needs of some of the most vulnerable people in his city.

Yes, there are some highly materialistic and selfish people who work only to serve their own desires, but most people aren't like that. In addition to being able to meet their financial needs and goals, most people want to have a significant and positive impact on others. Even those who don't find the specific tasks involved in their job meaningful often derive meaning from their work simply because it helps them support their families.

In the United States and other affluent nations, we tend to place a lot of emphasis on finding a job or career path that we feel passionate about or feel a calling to. This is a benefit of living in a free, prosperous, and economically dynamic nation. Many of us have the luxury of being able to seek jobs we believe will fit our interests and talents, although this isn't the case for everyone. For millions (if not billions) of people worldwide, work is meaningful simply because it means feeding and clothing their children and caring for their family members.

All this is to say that despite the unique ways people find meaning, what makes the pursuit of meaning similar for everyone around the world, in rich and poor countries alike, is that it's highly social. My research team has conducted studies in which we ask people from all walks of life to describe what makes their lives meaningful, and the most common response is family and other close relationships.[2]

The more socially connected people are, the more meaningful they feel.

When people mention other sources of meaning—religion, for example—most of the time they quickly reference relationships. They say, for instance, that their religious faith gives them meaning because it involves a relationship with the divine and a community of fellow believers. Even when people pray alone, they are engaged in an effort to socially connect (albeit in this case with a supernatural being). And they often pray for other people or for guidance with matters involving other people.

In 2021, the Pew Research Center conducted an international survey examining how people in different nations around the world find meaning in life.[3] For most nations, family is the most frequently mentioned source of meaning in life. Even in the United States, which is often described as the most materialistic and individualistic country in the world, Pew found that family and friends ranked higher than material wealth on what is most important to meaning. Most Americans care more about being socially rich than financially rich.

Studies have also found that the more socially connected people are, the more meaningful they feel.[4] Loneliness and social isolation make people feel meaningless. This is why ostracism has been referred to as social death. When people feel excluded or rejected, their sense of meaning in life plummets.

In addition, research finds that parents report higher levels of meaning than people who don't have children, and that parents experience the highest levels of meaning when they engage in activities that involve taking care of their kids.[5] Parenting can be stressful, but having children is a powerful way to understand that one is socially valued because children depend on their caregivers to thrive. Of course, people who don't have children clearly find meaning in their lives, especially if they're doing something that helps others flourish.

Meaninglessness Makes You Nostalgic

Since nostalgia involves people's cherished social memories, my colleagues and I reasoned that nostalgia plays an important role in helping people find, maintain, and restore meaning in life. To explore this, we tested whether people turn to nostalgia when life feels meaningless. If nostalgia is a meaning-making resource, as we assumed, when people face situations that make them doubt the meaningfulness of their lives, they should become more nostalgic.

Life is full of experiences that challenge our sense of meaning. The loss of a job, being betrayed by a romantic partner or close friend, failing to achieve a life goal, having the validity of a cherished belief questioned, and many other experiences that disrupt our expectations about the world and our place in it can threaten our perceptions of meaning.

As discussed in the previous chapter, the awareness of mortality is a particularly potent challenge to our sense of meaning, but it's just one existential threat. People turn to nostalgia to help them cope with the existential threat of death awareness, but do other threats to meaning similarly inspire nostalgia?

To find out, my colleagues and I first conducted a study to see if people became more nostalgic after pondering the potential meaninglessness of life.[6] To encourage people to think deeply about this, we randomly assigned participants to read a philosophical essay that focused on the cosmic insignificance of humans. The essay presented information about how (relative to the timeline of the universe or even our own planet) people have existed for but a brief moment. Participants in the control condition read an essay focused on the limitations of computers. This essay was selected based on previous work to resemble the "meaning threat" essay in length and how engaging readers found it to be. In other words, both essays were judged by readers to be intellectually stimulating, but only one essay encouraged readers to question the meaningfulness of human existence.

After participants read one of the two essays, they completed a nostalgia questionnaire. The results of the study supported the proposal that meaninglessness inspires nostalgia. Participants who read an essay about the insignificance of human life reported significantly higher levels of nostalgia than those who read an essay about the limitations of computers.

Most people probably don't sit around contemplating their potential cosmic insignificance. Between work, taking care of kids, socializing with friends and family, dealing with daily hassles, and trying to find a little time to pursue hobbies, most of us probably aren't all that interested in thinking about how tiny and transient we are in the grand scheme of things. That being said, we do hold beliefs about the world and other people that give us meaning, and occasionally those beliefs are challenged in a way that threatens meaning.

Disillusionment is the unhappiness we feel when an important belief is discredited. Feeling disillusioned undermines our perceptions of meaning. When we feel disillusioned, it means that we've lost faith or hope in something we once found meaningful. If disillusionment undercuts meaning and people become nostalgic when they lack meaning, feeling disillusioned should make people feel nostalgic.

A team of researchers led by Paul Maher, a professor of psychology at the University of Limerick in Ireland, recently tested this hypothesis.[7] To create feelings of disillusionment, the researchers randomly assigned participants to a writing task in which they were provided with a definition of disillusionment. They were then instructed to write about a major issue happening in the world that made them feel disillusioned. Participants in a control condition were instead instructed to write about an ordinary life experience. After this task, all participants were asked to write about a memory from their past and to indicate how nostalgic they felt. The researchers predicted that disillusionment would incline people to become nostalgic when reflecting on the past and that's exactly what they found.

Participants who were prompted to feel disillusioned became more nostalgic than those who weren't.

Thinking about our cosmic insignificance or a major issue in the world that makes us feel disillusioned are significant existential challenges, but it doesn't take something that deep to make us feel less meaningful. As it turns out, even something as subtle as feeling bored can threaten meaning.

Boredom is characterized by the feeling that we're not currently engaged in meaningful activities. As a result, when we're bored, our minds automatically start looking for ways to find meaning. Researchers examining the existential nature of boredom find that the search for meaning triggered by boredom can lead to both negative and positive activities.[8] On the negative side, boredom has been found to increase political extremism and has also been correlated with rioting. On the positive, boredom is associated with charitable giving, especially if the charity is perceived as one that makes a meaningful difference in the world. In short, boredom is an unpleasant state that signals a lack of meaning, which inspires people to get out of that state and do something that feels more consequential.

Since boredom makes people feel meaningless and motivates a search for meaning, and people become more nostalgic when their meaning is threatened, a research team led by Wijnand A. P. van Tilburg at the University of Essex in the UK proposed that boredom would increase nostalgia.

To test this, the research team used a clever tactic for making research participants feel bored.[9] They gave the participants a list of references about concrete mixtures and asked them to write down ten of them. No offense to scientists who study concrete, but most people would probably find the scientific and technical literature on concrete to be more than a little boring. The researchers were counting on this. In another condition, participants were only asked to write down two of the references.

Participants then wrote about a past memory and completed a nostalgia questionnaire. Just as the researchers predicted, participants who were asked to write down ten references about concrete mixtures subsequently became more nostalgic than participants who were only asked to write down two. In this experiment, the more boring task inspired more nostalgia.

I suspect boredom played a big role in the increased nostalgia many felt during the COVID-19 pandemic. Social isolation and loneliness were major drivers of nostalgia because people were stuck at home more than usual. The general anxiety and uncertainty people experienced also inspired nostalgia, but boredom likely also played a leading role, especially in places where there were long shutdowns and major disruptions to work and community life.

These are just a few examples of studies showing that when people's sense of meaning is compromised, they become more nostalgic. Cosmic insignificance, disillusionment, and boredom represent only a small list of meaning threats. Others discussed in previous chapters include loneliness and social exclusion, which are powerful threats to meaning given how central close relationships are to finding and sustaining meaning in life.

Nostalgia Increases Meaning

Meaninglessness inspires nostalgia, but does nostalgia increase meaning? My colleagues and I have conducted dozens of experiments showing that when people are prompted to engage in nostalgia, they subsequently report higher levels of meaning in life.[10] Other researchers have used a number of different nostalgia inductions to find similar results.[11] Activities that help you revisit cherished memories, such as writing about a nostalgic memory, listening to nostalgic music, and traveling somewhere that inspires nostalgia have been found to lead to a greater sense of meaning in life.

Nostalgia doesn't just increase meaning; it also restores meaning. Remember the research showing that boredom increases nostalgia? Having people copy a bunch of references about concrete made them bored and feel more meaningless, and it also made them more nostalgic. The researchers conducted additional studies to see if the nostalgia that was triggered by boredom restored meaning.[12] It did. People turn to nostalgia when they're bored because nostalgia makes life feel more meaningful.

Other studies similarly indicate that nostalgia counters experiences that threaten meaning by reminding people of experiences that generated meaning in the past. This pulls people out of that current of meaninglessness and reminds them that even though life can at times feel pointless, it's also full of experiences that are meaningful.

In one of my studies, an older male participant described a memory involving taking his kids to their first professional baseball game. What was interesting about his narrative is that he wrote that he sometimes doubted that he amounted to much in his life but that it was memories like this that reminded him that he worked hard to have close relationships with his kids when they were growing up because he wasn't close to his own father. When he thought about his relationships with his children, he felt like he had accomplished something important. He helped give his children a happy childhood.

> **Nostalgia boosts meaning by focusing our attention on the social relationships that give us meaning.**

Nostalgia Focuses the Mind on Meaningful Social Relationships

Meaning comes from feeling like we're making important contributions to the lives of others. Given this and the fact that nostalgia is highly social in nature, it shouldn't come as a surprise that nostalgia boosts meaning by focusing our attention on the social relationships that give us meaning.

When my colleagues and I tested the effect of nostalgia on meaning, we also measured how socially connected people feel. Using statistical techniques that allowed us to examine the relationship between nostalgia, social connectedness, and meaning, we were able to test if the connection between nostalgia and meaning is attributable to the increased feelings of social connectedness that nostalgia provides. We found that it is.

Nostalgia directs our attention to past meaningful social experiences. By doing this, nostalgia focuses our minds on the importance of social relationships. Importantly, this promotes meaning because nostalgic memories are not just everyday social memories; we're not typically nostalgic about memories that don't implicate our own social significance. For example, even if you enjoy going to the dentist for a routine cleaning, you probably aren't nostalgic about that experience, even if it was perfectly pleasant and you truly like your dentist and hygienist. This is because going to the dentist doesn't necessarily make us feel socially significant.

A lot of day-to-day social encounters are fairly passive. They don't involve us doing something that really matters or they don't include the people who make us feel like we truly matter. But nostalgic memories are different. This is why we're often nostalgic for holidays such as Christmas, Hanukkah, Ramadan, Independence Day, and Thanksgiving; special occasions such as weddings and graduations; and vacations with loved ones. These are the types of social memories that make us think about the deep relationships that make us feel that we matter.

Even when these memories involve people who are no longer alive or those we no longer have a relationship with, they're useful for finding meaning in the present. First, they remind us that meaning is about relationships, and we need these reminders from time to time. Second, they offer meaning-making lessons for current relationships.

Perhaps you have nostalgic memories about baking cookies with your grandmother, but she's no longer alive. Even though you can't talk to her anymore, and even if you have no desire to bake cookies in the present, I suspect if you drill a little deeper into those memories, you'll discover that it wasn't the particular activity of baking that mattered as much as it was an opportunity to spend quality time with someone who deeply mattered to you. This could inspire you to think about ways to create space for that kind of quality time with people you're close to now or people you'd like to be closer to.

Regular nostalgic exercises such as nostalgic journaling, scrapbooking, or other creative activities can be helpful ways to focus your mind on what makes life meaningful. They're especially good ways to focus your mind on social significance.

Bring to mind a nostalgic memory from your life. Specifically try to think about how this memory reveals what you find meaningful in life. How does the meaning you find in this memory relate to other people? How does it make you feel socially significant? If you're experiencing a sense of meaning-lessness, how might this memory help you affirm or restore a sense of meaning?

Summary Notes for "Nostalgia Focuses You on What Gives You Meaning"

- We humans are driven to perceive the social dimensions of life as meaningful. Our social needs involve a lifelong quest to matter.

- Our high level of self-awareness directs us to make sense of the world around us, but it also causes us to make sense of our internal experience of being alive.

- Having a strong sense of meaning usually involves feeling like we're doing things that matter in the world.

- When we perceive our lives as full of meaning, we're less likely to suffer from mental illness and destructive behavior and more inclined to practice healthy lifestyles. We're also more engaged and energized socially.

- Even something as seemingly insignificant as boredom can encourage us to feel a lack of meaning. In these cases, nostalgia can help us regain a sense of meaning.

CHAPTER 12

NOSTALGIA INSPIRES EXISTENTIAL AGENCY

Years ago, William Dunn encountered a young boy who was having behavioral problems. After learning that the boy's father wasn't in his life, William offered to take the young man fishing. For William, fishing had always been a restorative activity that helped him deal with the stressors of life, and fishing also had a personal nostalgic connection. Although his own childhood had been difficult, William still cherished memories of fishing with his father, and he'd always known how special it was when his dad took him fishing. William's fishing outings with the young man became regular events, and soon the boy's behavior started to improve. He became a better student and was more respectful to his mother at home.

After seeing such a positive change in this boy's life, it became William's life calling to help other fatherless kids. He started contacting foster homes and taking groups of kids fishing every weekend, at his own expense. William did this for years—helping kids learn not just how to fish but also how to take responsibility in life and how to support one another.

A few years ago, William was able to take his calling to the next level by establishing Take a Kid Fishing Inc. as a nonprofit organization, allowing him to expand his mission of mentoring underprivileged and fatherless kids through fishing trips. William still goes fishing with the first boy—now a young man—whom he helped over a decade ago.

William took a hobby shaped by his own nostalgia and turned it into a project that has directly improved the lives of thousands of kids and has likely indirectly affected the lives of many more, because the kids William has helped will be motivated to do the same by the nostalgic memories William helped them create. Every day, people like William all over the world act with purpose to change the lives of others for the better.

Earlier in the book I discussed how nostalgia motivates prosocial behavior. In this chapter, I want to dig deeper into the existential nature of nostalgia-motivated prosocial behavior by focusing on human agency and, more specifically, what I refer to as *existential agency*—the belief that we have the power to live a meaningful life.

Nostalgia makes us feel more meaningful. It also helps us see that meaning in life is within our control, that meaning requires taking ownership over our own existence. Furthermore, nostalgia helps us understand that meaning involves action, and the most meaning-affirming actions are the ones that serve others. Nostalgia orients us toward such service. To truly live a meaningful life, we must fully embrace our existential agency and use it to contribute to our families, communities, and the broader world.

What Is Existential Agency and Why Is It Important?

A number of aspects in life are out of our control. We can't choose who our parents are, the country of our birth, our physical characteristics, or many of our psychological traits. Genetics, as well as the social and cultural environments we don't have much say in, significantly influence who we are.

An agentic life involves making mistakes and learning from them.

That being said, humans are an intellectual species and that means we have the power to generate long-term goals and follow through with thoughtful planning and determination. We can consciously decide to build upon our strengths and limit the impact of our weaknesses. For instance, if you know that you're likely to eat too much junk food if it's in the house, you have the power to plan accordingly, to purchase healthier options in the store, and to do whatever else it takes to reduce temptation at home. Indeed, this is a key feature of finding success in conquering addiction. Even when we have genetic vulnerabilities, knowledge is power. Knowing our vulnerabilities and triggers gives us important knowledge that we can use to plan, make informed decisions, and structure our lives in ways that best position us to achieve our goals.

If we do get derailed, our agency can empower us to reset, get back on course, or find a new path. An agentic life involves making mistakes and learning from them. It also entails experimentation and figuring out how different environments and people affect our emotions, thoughts, and behaviors. An agentic life involves running all sorts of mental simulations, traveling into the past and future, and using personal and collective experience to move toward the lives we most want to lead.

When it comes to finding meaning in life, we're not merely at the mercy of good or bad fortune. We don't have to let others determine our existential fates. Regardless of the cards we're dealt and the life circumstances we find ourselves in, we're all in the driver's seat when it comes to finding meaning. To be existentially agentic is to take responsibility for finding, maintaining, and restoring meaning.

Andrew Abeyta and I coined the term *existential agency* a few years ago because we thought it was important to highlight and study the motivational and self-regulatory nature of meaning. Plenty of people in the field of psychology were studying meaning and how it contributes to overall mental and physical health, but few had explicitly focused on the agentic nature of meaning.

My own thinking on existential agency has been largely influenced by the work of the Austrian psychiatrist Viktor Frankl. As a prisoner in a Nazi concentration camp during World War II, Frankl witnessed and experienced unimaginable suffering. Even so, he developed an appreciation for the power of psychological freedom and the agency it creates. Frankl's book *Man's Search for Meaning* details his experiences in the concentration camps as well as the existential psychotherapy he developed as a result. He writes,

We who lived in concentration camps can remember the men who walked through the huts comforting others, giving away their last piece of bread. They may have been few in number, but they offer sufficient proof that everything can be taken from a man but one thing: the last of the human freedoms—to choose one's own attitude in any given set of circumstances, to choose one's own way.[1]

Frankl argued that meaning in life is a fundamental human need and also that individuals have the freedom to pursue a meaningful life—regardless of how difficult that life is. People may fail to take responsibility for their lives, but that doesn't mean they don't have the ability to do so. It just means that they aren't acting on their agency.

Existential agency is the self-regulatory component of meaning. It's us taking meaning into our own hands. This doesn't conflict with other perspectives on meaning—for example, a religious perspective that suggests meaning is a gift from a divine creator—because even if you believe that God has a purpose for your life, I suspect you also believe that it's your responsibility to uncover that purpose and act on it, regardless of the barriers that may stand in your way. You understand that if you want to reach your full potential, you are ultimately the one who has to step up.

Regardless of whether you believe that you're designed with a purpose, it's clear that most of us long for meaning in life, and all of us are uniquely equipped with the ability to take responsibility for living a meaningful life.

Nostalgia Inspires an Existentially Agentic Mindset

To be existentially agentic, we need to be aware of and embrace our psychological freedom. Existentially agentic action starts with an existentially agentic mindset. Nostalgia supports this mindset.

Remember, nostalgia helps us refocus our attention on what we find most central to our self-concept. Life is full of distractions, and we often operate on autopilot. This can be helpful after we've established the types of habits and routines that support our health and well-being, but it can also be detrimental if our behaviors are mindless or harmful. Relying too much on autopilot can also prove a barrier to living a more intentional life. At least some of the time, we need to take stock of our lives and ask ourselves if we're optimizing our psychological freedom. We need to refocus our attention and activate an existentially agentic mindset. This is where nostalgia can be especially useful.

When people engage in nostalgic reflection, they access the memories that reveal the authentic self—the person they truly want to be. This helps them identify a goal, which is the first step to using one's existential agency to make a positive life change. For example, a common meaning-focused goal involves spending more time with family. Imagine someone

> **Nostalgic reflection leads to increased motivation to pursue the life goals that people find most meaningful.**

who has moved far away from their family to pursue a particular career. They've lived at a distance for years but have recently felt like something is missing, despite enjoying a great deal of professional success. They begin to revisit nostalgic memories that involve the family they moved away from, the relationships that make them feel truly valued. This offers clarity for future planning. They decide they're going to start thinking about new ways to market the skills they have developed to find a new job closer to family, even though it will be difficult to change jobs. It might even require a pay cut or doing something quite a bit different from what they are currently doing. When they begin to have doubts about moving closer to their family when faced with so much upheaval and uncertainty, they return to the nostalgic memories of time they spent with their family. This keeps that meaningful goal fresh in their mind, which reenergizes them. It renews their focus and motivation to pursue their goal and inspires them to think creatively about this challenge. Nostalgia helps them maintain hope and reminds them that the things in life that are most meaningful often don't come easy.

A number of studies have found that nostalgic reflection leads to increased motivation to pursue the life goals that people find most meaningful. For example, in a series of experiments led by Constantine Sedikides at the University of Southampton in the UK, participants were instructed to spend a few minutes writing about a nostalgic or an ordinary memory.[2] They were then instructed to list their most important current goal and least important current goal. Finally, they were asked how motivated they were to pursue these goals. The researchers found that nostalgia increased people's motivation to pursue their most important goal, but not their least.

In other words, nostalgia doesn't simply make us more motivated to engage in any action. It specifically motivates us to work toward the goals we view as most important to our lives. Nostalgia focuses our mental energy on the activities that give us the most meaning.

In one of my studies, a research participant shared a nostalgic memory about college graduation and how it was such an important memory because he was the first person in his family to attend college. He also noted that he reflected on this memory whenever he doubted himself and lost his motivation to finish the PhD he was currently working toward. He wrote that the memory helped him refocus on his goal to complete his degree so that he could pursue his dream of being a college professor and inspiring other first-generation students to pursue their goals, in turn.

It's normal to sometimes feel a loss of control over life. When you feel like you're not living how you truly want to live or that you're not in control, nostalgia can help you harness your power by inspiring an existentially agentic mindset. In these circumstances, use nostalgia to take a step back and recalibrate. Bring to mind a cherished nostalgic memory. Focus your mind on what this memory can tell you about the life you want to live. Ask yourself how it can help you make plans to move toward living the life you want. Are there specific steps you can take, even small ones, to start regaining control over your life?

Existential Agency as
Outward-Oriented Well-Being

The fact that meaning has an agentic component, that it involves us making decisions and acting on them, reveals something else important about our existential health. Meaning is much more than a self-reflective mental state. Meaning is about action. When we have a greater sense of existential agency, we become more engaged in life. As the story of William Dunn and Take a Kid Fishing Inc. highlights, meaning is about making a decision to do something meaningful and then rolling up one's sleeves and doing it.

This also means that meaning is different from mental states we often associate with well-being, such as happiness. When psychologists study well-being, they focus on more inward-looking mental states. They ask questions such as "Do you currently feel happy? Sad? Anxious? Depressed? Stressed? How satisfied are you with your life? Your relationships? Your job? How often do you feel lonely?" and so on. These are certainly important questions, but if we truly want to understand human well-being, we need to understand how thoughts and feelings turn into behaviors.

We all know from experience that people act differently depending on their mood. I remember reading about a clever study years ago in which researchers ran an experiment at a bar that involved attaching a card with a joke on it to the bills of some of the patrons.[3] The basic idea was that making customers smile when receiving their bill would make them more generous. To test this, half of the bills given to customers came with a small card containing a joke, but the other half didn't. The researchers found that when paying for their drinks, patrons who received the joke card tipped more.

This isn't a surprising finding, especially to anyone who's ever worked a job in which success depends on customer satisfaction. There's a reason why businesses spend a considerable amount of time and money trying to understand and improve customer service—a happy customer is more likely to be a long-term customer.

But appreciating that psychological states influence behavior isn't the same as thinking about behavior as being part of well-being.

Most psychologists treat behaviors as separate from well-being. I don't. I think our actions are a central part of our well-being. This is an important point, in my opinion, because if we view well-being purely in terms of inward-focused mental states, we overemphasize the importance of feeling good while underemphasizing the significance of doing good. And doing good is often what ultimately makes us feel good.

Behavior influences our inward-focused feelings just as much as these feelings influence our behavior. In addition, feelings and actions aren't always immediately aligned. Sometimes good behavior—behavior that's healthy for us or helpful to others—doesn't feel so good, at least not at first.

Physical exercise is a tangible example. Increasingly, people are understanding that working out benefits both physical and mental health. But to get the benefits of exercise, people obviously have to do the behavior of exercise, whether they feel like it or not. When people are feeling down and demotivated, or just feeling lazy, they typically don't want to exercise. Additionally, when you're out of shape, exercise doesn't exactly feel good.

A more holistic view of well-being would include not just behavior but also actions directed toward helping others and improving the world.

In the short term, the positive behavior of exercise is often associated with negative psychological and physical states. The benefits of exercising come later. Eventually, after getting in shape, regular exercise boosts positive mood and improves mental health more broadly. Thus exercise is a behavior that's indicative of positive well-being, even if it doesn't feel good at the time. But this perspective requires a more action-oriented view of well-being, one that treats well-being as more than how people feel and considers how they behave.

Well-being isn't just self-serving; it reflects our engagement in the world around us. It's important to take care of ourselves, but that's just one part of well-being. Because the success of our species relies on social cooperation, and because meaning in life is found in our belief that we matter—that we're making a significant difference in the lives of others—I think well-being is also very much about our actions in the social world.

Even if you do a wonderful job of taking care of your health and well-being by exercising, eating healthy, getting plenty of sleep, and so on, you'll feel incomplete if you aren't engaged in activities that serve others. Indeed, there's a large body of research documenting the mental and physical health benefits of volunteer work and other prosocial behaviors.[4] A more holistic view of well-being would include not just behavior but also actions directed toward helping others and improving the world. Existential agency orients us toward outward-focused action. As Viktor Frankl articulated in his example of the concentration-camp prisoners who gave away their last piece of bread to others, agency is at its best and most inspiring when people look beyond their self-interest, even in the most difficult situations.

When people view themselves as responsible for finding meaning in life, they don't turn inward; they turn outward. They don't simply ruminate; they act. Pondering major existential questions—such as whether humans are cosmically insignificant—might be an interesting philosophical exercise, but when it comes to actually living in a way that feels meaningful, people have to get out of their heads and into the world.

Nostalgia Supports Existentially Agentic, Outward-Oriented Well-Being

Nostalgia doesn't just make people feel good; it inspires them to do good. It fuels the type of existential agency that drives people to positively impact the world. Remember that nostalgia makes people feel socially connected and also motivates them to reach out to others. Nostalgia isn't just an agency-promoting resource that helps people meet their social needs. It also encourages them to want to help others.

Think about creative inspiration. Musicians, filmmakers, writers, entrepreneurs, and others who are in the business of trying to innovate or do something unique often have experienced something in their lives that inspires their creative work. Even when people strive for novelty, they need their creativity sparked by something, and often it's something they find personally meaningful from their past. They might be creating entirely new characters or developing an original world for those characters to inhabit, but below the surface of their art is a deeper connection to real-world elements of their past. Creativity and innovation are, in my opinion, indicators of outward-focused well-being. When people make something to share with the world, they're engaged in the type of activity that cultivates dynamic and flourishing societies.

People who start businesses are trying to make money. A business won't last long if it doesn't turn a profit. But most entrepreneurs aren't primarily focused on making money. They're also motivated to serve an unmet need in their community, introduce a product or service that will improve people's lives, or find a way to turn a talent or hobby into something that interests others. Entrepreneurship is action. It starts with an idea but it requires outward-oriented action to be successful.

Entrepreneurship is also often stressful and anxiety-provoking because it involves taking chances. Some people leave stable jobs with satisfying incomes to strike out on their own, and many put their own money at risk. All entrepreneurship requires putting something out there that could fail. From a purely inward-focused view of well-being, entrepreneurial behavior doesn't make sense, but from an outward-oriented view, entrepreneurship is a powerful indicator of well-being because it reveals someone engaged in an activity that will impact the lives of others.

This doesn't mean all entrepreneurial activities are beneficial for society. Some business ventures take advantage of people's vulnerabilities and are motivated purely by self-interest, but I don't think this characterizes most entrepreneurship. Look around your community and you'll find all sorts of people trying to make a living or just a little extra money selling products and services that make your life more pleasant and the community a better place to live.

For many entrepreneurs, nostalgia plays a role in their business. Someone who opens a new ice-cream shop may have powerful memories of their mother taking them to get ice cream as a special after-school treat. Someone who opens up a food truck may be inspired to share favorite foods from their childhood. Another who trains to be a mechanic with the goal of starting their own shop may have developed their love for working on cars as the result of happy memories fixing up old cars with their dad. I've met all sorts of small-business owners who have nostalgic stories that sparked their start-up ambitions.

Of course, many people are creators of some type but aren't necessarily looking to make money. Even so, they still use their talents to positively impact others. They sew quilts for family members, sing in their church choir, use their talents to help an organization raise money for a good cause, and so on. Such activities are often tied to nostalgic memories. People are more likely to want to develop and share their gifts if they're associated with nostalgic memories.

In one of my studies, a research participant wrote about a nostalgic memory involving her mother teaching her how to quilt. She discussed how she wasn't really that interested in quilting and thought the quilts her mom and others made were too old-fashioned. They didn't reflect what she was into. But she loved spending that time with her mom, and those memories inspired her to make more modern-looking quilts that she liked better, and so she developed a quilting practice that she was better able to enjoy with her mom.

All of us are potential creators who can positively affect others. Even something as simple as baking cookies to share with neighbors is an agentic and outward-focused activity often rooted in nostalgia. Baking cookies for a neighbor is motivated by a desire to do something kind, something that will make someone else feel happy and socially valued. What makes us think that baking them cookies will have that effect? In all likelihood, it's because we have fond memories of someone making cookies for us. When a family member, friend, or neighbor did so, it made us feel welcomed and valued. Cookies are made of flour, sugar, fat, and nostalgia.

Nostalgia can help you identify and take advantage of your creative potential in ways that improve the world around you. Bring to mind a nostalgic memory that involves using your creative abilities. How might this memory help you find ways to create or innovate today?

Summary Notes for "Nostalgia Inspires Existential Agency"

- Existential agency is the belief that we have the power to lead a meaningful life. It's the self-regulatory aspect of meaning.

- Living an agentic life means that we actively use our experience to take responsibility for discovering, maintaining, and restoring meaning.

- Nostalgic reflection aids existential agency because it reminds us of who we truly want to be. Nostalgia also reminds us of the activities that bring us the most meaning.

- Our behavior influences our feelings just as much as our feelings affect our behavior.

- When we view ourselves as responsible for the meaning we find in life, we don't simply turn inward; we also act to help others. Nostalgia helps us meet our social needs, but it also encourages us to benefit others.

PART 5

USING THE PAST TO BUILD A BETTER FUTURE

CHAPTER 13

NOSTALGIA HELPS YOU NAVIGATE A FAST-MOVING WORLD

I recently switched from a gas-powered lawn mower to a battery-powered one. To be honest, it was my wife's idea. I was skeptical of making the change because I've been mowing lawns with a traditional gas mower for decades. I was comfortable with the technology I knew and wasn't motivated to make a change. What if the electric mower wouldn't perform as well? What if the battery didn't last long enough? My concerns weren't based on evidence but in the uncertainty that often accompanies change. Now that I've switched over, I love it. No more messing with gasoline. No spark plugs or oil to change. It's quieter, easy to store, does a great job, and is much better for the environment. In fact, I've been so impressed that I started replacing my old power tools with handy electric versions.

Looking back, I wonder why I was so resistant to change. I consider myself a fairly open-minded person who appreciates technological progress. Plus, switching to an electric mower isn't exactly a major life decision. Worst-case scenario, if I tried going electric and I didn't like it, I'd only be out a few hundred dollars.

Change is an essential aspect of life. Improving our situation and the world around us requires a willingness to explore new ideas and possibilities, to experiment with doing things differently. Although some of us embrace novelty better than others, change is often difficult. Even among the most adventurous among us, a world that changes too dramatically or quickly can cause a lot of anxiety, and a certain amount of fear of change is probably healthy. The problem is that too much caution or fear of transformation can hinder personal growth and societal progress. It can also prove harmful in situations that require being able to quickly adapt to new circumstances.

Nostalgia can help people properly manage their anxiety and adapt to a changing environment. As a driver of progress, nostalgia cultivates the type of mindset we need to solve compelling problems and create a better future.

Why Change Is Difficult

As discussed earlier, we want to have the sense that our self is relatively stable across time. Although we desire growth (and the change it requires), we also don't want to lose our core sense of self. This desire for self-continuity isn't exclusive to our self-concepts; we also prefer the world around us to remain stable.

Remember that people are motivated by security needs *and* growth needs. We naturally want to avoid danger. This is why stability matters and change is so difficult. When the world around us is predictable, we can build up the type of knowledge that allows us to safely navigate and thrive within our environment. If the world around us is frequently fluctuating, we can't rely on our built-up expectations about how the world works; we must learn new ideas, rules, and patterns. Change creates uncertainty and thus the potential for anxiety, especially when we think change has the potential to harm us in some way. Social and cultural transformation can be particularly anxiety-provoking because successfully navigating our social world is so vital to our survival and well-being.

Have you ever traveled to a different part of the world and experienced anxiety caused by dramatically different social customs? Have you ever experienced a situation in your own culture in which you entered a social environment that was foreign to you? Did feeling out of place stress you out or make you nervous?

In a diverse and dynamic country such as the United States, social and cultural transformation can happen fairly quickly, and that can make people uncomfortable and anxious. It's easy to dismiss other people's concerns about change if it doesn't affect our own lives much, but we're all vulnerable to anxiety caused by the uncertainty of transition, especially if we've been comfortable in our current social environment.

It isn't all that difficult to embrace new technology when we're the ones seeking it out or when we have a clear idea of how it will make our lives easier. Many of us look forward to the new upgrades and gadgets that streamline and simplify daily tasks, but technological progress can also cause a great deal of distress. For instance, lots of people fear automation because of the disruption it causes to employment. They worry that robots and computers will eliminate the need for certain jobs, which makes it hard for some people to meet their financial needs and to feel like meaningful contributors to society. This isn't a new fear, of course. Technological innovation has long caused people to worry—often with good reason—how change might take away people's livelihoods and significance.

The automatic teller machine (ATM) was introduced in the 1970s, and the number of ATMs has increased dramatically in the decades since. Many feared these machines would kill jobs by eliminating the need for human bank tellers, because you wouldn't need people to count and dispense money if a machine could do the job. Contrary to those fears, the number of human tellers has actually increased. Although ATMs decreased the number of bank tellers needed at a given bank branch, this new technology also made it cheaper for banks to open new branches, which led to hiring even more tellers. As a result, banking is now more convenient than ever because there are more branches and ATMs. In addition, ATMs performing simple tasks meant that the people banks hired could be trained to focus more on building relationships with clients and offering additional services.

Automation doesn't always create more jobs. The latest threat to bank employment has come from online banking, which was already growing in popularity before the pandemic. Many people who were initially skeptical of online banking have now converted to it out of health concerns regarding COVID-19 or because their local bank branch closed its lobby during the pandemic. As more and more people discover how efficient online banking is, there may be a decreased need for human workers at bank branches—and we may need fewer physical banks.

Even if automation ultimately reduces the number of traditional bank jobs, the broader history of automation thus far suggests that new jobs will develop. This doesn't make it easy for people who lose work and therefore need to find a new job or learn new skills. Unfortunately, even when change is largely beneficial, it can still generate significant disruption, uncertainty, and anxiety.

Why Change Is Important

Change isn't inherently good or bad. Consider technological advances in food production and distribution. Thanks to progress on this front, people in many parts of the world are at far less risk of starvation. Additionally, the modern world faces the associated challenges of obesity, food waste, and the damage that comes with factory farming, all while offering a good portion of us healthier food at cheaper prices. In other words, change is complex. Technological advancements that make it easier for us to grow, secure, and access food have solved some problems while creating others. Clearly we must consider the big picture, rethink our behavior, and keep changing.

There's no way to predict all the positive and negative consequences of experimentation and innovation, but we'd never have a shot of improving our lives or the lives of others around the world if we rejected change outright. This means that we need resources to help us navigate a changing world as wisely as possible.

Nostalgia as a Resource for Managing the Anxiety Caused by Change

As I've discussed throughout this book, when we experience negative psychological states, our minds naturally turn to nostalgia for comfort. For instance, when we feel lonely, we tend to recall nostalgic memories that makes us feel loved and supported. Nostalgia has a soothing effect when we're socially distressed.

The same thing happens when we feel anxious about a changing world. If a company adopts a new technology for its workers that requires them to learn a whole new way of doing their jobs, it's common for the employees to initially feel frustrated and anxious and to then feel nostalgic about the way things used to be at work. In such circumstances, it's tempting to view nostalgia as a barrier to adapting to change. If only people would stop dwelling on the past, adopt a more positive attitude, and embrace the new way of doing things, the company could get everyone trained more quickly and move forward with the new system.

> Nostalgia helps to slow things down, which gives people time to process and make sense of the change.

But people don't work that way. We aren't robots, and nostalgia isn't the barrier people often think it is. When we turn to nostalgia in response to change, we aren't necessarily rejecting change; our brains are working to help us adapt to a new reality at a pace we can handle psychologically. When company employees engage in nostalgia about the way things used to be, it typically means that they're talking to other employees. Critically, what they're doing is helping comfort one another. On the surface, the nostalgia they share may appear to be a rejection of change, but in reality, nostalgia is often a tool for people to talk through changes with one another and ease their way into a new way of doing business. Nostalgia helps to slow things down, which gives people time to process and make sense of the change.

Melinda Milligan, a sociology professor at Sonoma State University in California, documented this firsthand in a field study in which she observed and interviewed employees of a coffee shop before and after the business moved to a new location.[1] To gain a deeper understanding of how employees managed this change, Milligan took a job at the coffee shop prior to its relocation and observed her fellow employees for nearly two years, which included four months at the old coffee shop and eighteen months at the new one. During this time, she observed and engaged in conversations with her fellow employees to get a sense of their thoughts and feelings during the transition. Following the observation period, she conducted in-depth interviews to more carefully examine the effects of the relocation.

Milligan found that employees often engaged in nostalgia after the coffee shop moved. They talked among themselves about their nostalgia, sharing stories about memories from the old shop. Change triggered nostalgia. Critically, Milligan also observed that nostalgia helped the employees adjust to their new work setting. Nostalgia offered them psychological comfort and stability during a period of transition.

Employers could therefore welcome nostalgia and try to help their workers use it to reduce anxiety. Keep in mind that when people are anxious, they're far less likely to be open-minded and prepared to learn. Anxiety makes people more rigid and defensive. It's a major barrier to people accepting change. If nostalgia has a soothing effect, it will help people become more emotionally prepared for change.

If you're going through a difficult change in your life that's causing you stress or anxiety, try keeping a nostalgia journal for a while. Each day, spend a few minutes writing about a nostalgic experience you find comforting. If the change you're experiencing involves other people, create a nostalgic social activity that allows you and others to share memories that can help you manage the anxiety associated with this change. Even something as simple as organizing a weekly lunch or happy hour in which everyone is encouraged not to just complain about the change but to discuss memories they experience together can help the group navigate the change.

Nostalgia as a Tool for Adapting to Change

We can't effectively adapt to change if we're too distressed to take on new information. Nostalgia helps us incorporate new information and employ it to make the types of decisions that will allow us to thrive in new environments and circumstances.

Remember, nostalgia focuses our mind on the experiences that have made our life feel meaningful. It also orients us toward the types of goals that help us find and sustain meaning. When the world around us is changing in important ways, we usually have big decisions to make. For instance, if there are major changes at our job that make us feel anxious, we need to decide if it's in our best interest to embrace the new reality at work or if we'd be better off looking for a different job. In the moment, it can be difficult to know whether the change will ultimately be a good fit, so it's critical that we're able to think clearly about what it is about the job that fits our goals and gives us meaning and whether that can be preserved.

Nostalgic memories about the job can offer clues. They remind us of what it is we most value. If one of the most important features of the job is relationships with coworkers, then our nostalgic memories will let us know. Will the changes at work affect those relationships? If not, then the change might be worth adapting to. But maybe what we most value at this job is autonomy. If the change happening is a threat to that autonomy, nostalgic reflection can help us determine that the change isn't going to work so well and that perhaps it's a good time to start looking for a job that's a better fit.

Ultimately nostalgia's capacity to help us adapt to change might be driven by nostalgia restoring a sense of agency or control. When our world is stable and predictable, we feel more confident in our ability to exercise control. We understand the variables we're working with. Major changes disrupt that.

Sometimes people reject transformation as a way to regain a sense of control, even if the change might be beneficial for them in the long run. Sticking with the job example, a change at work that makes employees experience a temporary feeling of lost control may help them develop new technical skills that serve their career advancement goals in the future, which will actually offer them more control over their futures. They just need a way to manage that sense of a lack of control so they can adapt to the change. By helping people feel agentic, nostalgia can help them feel less anxious and help them maintain the sense of control that makes them better positioned to adapt to a changing world.

A team of researchers led by Niwen Huang at Beijing Normal University in China examined nostalgia as a resource for restoring the feeling of control.[2] I found this research to be particularly interesting because the researchers focused on a technology-driven societal change that has quickly and dramatically impacted how people live: the widespread adoption of smartphones. They specifically focused on how smartphone technology can make people feel less in control.

Smartphones have obvious benefits. Having a powerful computer that fits in our pockets and allows us to be connected to the internet and other people at all times means we can get directions; book a flight, hotel room, or restaurant reservation; pay bills; conduct important business; access and listen to a nearly infinite catalog of music and other art; and accomplish countless other tasks from nearly anywhere. But it also means we're easily distracted. A 2022 survey found that Americans check their smartphones an average of 352 times per day.[3] Other studies have found that when people are regularly distracted by their smartphones, they find the activities they're otherwise engaged in to be less meaningful.[4]

Niwen Huang's research team proposed that smartphone use undermines people's sense of control over their lives, which leads people to turn to nostalgia as a way to restore that control. To test these ideas, Huang and his team conducted several experiments in which they brought groups together and had some people use their smartphones while others did not. They also conducted surveys in which they measured how frequently participants were using their smartphones throughout the day.

As predicted, the researchers found that participants who used their smartphones during social activities felt less in control than the participants who didn't. Similarly, they observed that the more frequently people use their smartphones throughout the day, the less they feel in control of their lives. The researchers also found that participants who used their smartphones during social activities felt more nostalgic than participants who did not. The more the participants used their smartphones throughout the day, the more nostalgic they felt. Moreover, Huang's team observed that the increased nostalgia that participants felt when using their smartphones was driven by the lost sense of control, and that nostalgia helped them regain some feeling of control.

Nostalgia can remind us that the experiences we truly cherish involve deeper social engagement.

Smartphones are another example of change that has both positive and negative effects. They can make life easier and more entertaining, but they can also distract us from important tasks and the experiences that make life feel meaningful. Similarly, there's growing concern about the potential role that the internet and social media play in societal problems such as political polarization. Social media is a powerful tool for connection, but it's also quite adept at spreading misinformation and promoting outrage. It also creates echo chambers in which people almost entirely interact with others who share their political and social views. All of this can make it difficult for people to come together and find common ground and for a society to sustain a unifying cultural narrative that inspires trust, tolerance, and civic participation.

If the internet is contributing to polarization, nostalgia might be a resource that can help us adapt to this changing digital world. If we are spending more and more time online interacting with those who share our beliefs and consuming media that makes us see the worst in those who don't, nostalgia can remind us that the experiences we truly cherish involve deeper social engagement.

If some of our nostalgic memories include people we disagree with on politics and other issues, nostalgia can help us better appreciate their full humanity. People are complex, and most of us have diverse perspectives on many issues. Even when someone supports politics you strongly disagree with, they probably have other beliefs or interests in common with you. Nostalgic memories involving that person can help reveal those commonalities.

Indeed, research has found that when people reflect on a nostalgic memory involving someone from another social group, their feelings toward that entire group become more positive. Rhiannon Turner, a professor of psychology at Queen's University in Belfast, and her colleagues found that having young adults reflect on a nostalgic memory involving older adults increased positive attitudes toward elders.[5] In other studies, Turner and her team similarly found that when people reflect on a nostalgic memory involving someone with a mental illness, they develop more positive feelings toward others who suffer from mental illness.[6]

Cultural nostalgic memories, even those concerning seemingly silly pop cultural topics, can serve as connecting points among people who have opposing beliefs. When individuals with different beliefs share nostalgic memories around sports, music, movies, fashion, and so on, they are reminded that life is much more than politics and that those who are demonized by hyperpartisan media are actual people with real-life stories, fears, hopes, and dreams.

If nostalgia can help people who have diverse viewpoints come together around shared experiences, it might prove an important resource for reducing polarization and helping people find common ground in order to build a better future for all.

If you are having conflict with people over politics and would like to find a way to seek common ground, try using nostalgia. You probably have nostalgic memories that include someone you disagree with on social or political issues. Spend a few minutes thinking about one of these memories. Is there something from it that reminds you of something you have in common with this person? How might this help you better appreciate the complexity of other people?

Summary Notes for "Nostalgia Helps You Navigate a Fast-Moving World"

- Change often causes anxiety. Some measure of caution about change is warranted, but too much fear can hinder personal and societal growth.

- Even when change is mostly beneficial, as in the case with many technological advances, it still creates uncertainty and anxiety.

- When we turn to nostalgia in the face of change, it doesn't mean that we're rejecting change; it means that our brains are helping us adapt to a new reality at a pace we can handle.

- Nostalgia helps us adapt to change by restoring our sense of agency or control.

- Nostalgic memories involving people we disagree with can bring us closer by highlighting our commonalities.

CONCLUSION

NOsTALGsA ANv THE
PsYCHOLOGY OF PROGREss

A few years ago, I attended a presentation by a professor who studies scientific, medical, and technological innovation. The presentation was specifically focused on different barriers to innovation, mostly political and other policy barriers that make it difficult for scientists, engineers, and entrepreneurs to create and bring to the market new products and services that have the potential to improve lives and help solve major societal and global challenges. He also discussed cultural and psychological barriers to progress—specifically, nostalgia. According to this expert, nostalgia is distinctly at odds with a progress mindset.

The presenter saw nostalgia as antithetical to progress because he imagined that it causes people to privilege the familiarity of the past over the possibilities of the future. His position is not unique. I regularly encounter advocates for progress who suggest that nostalgia is a formidable barrier to our efforts to improve the world. In their minds, you're either focused on the past or planning for the future, and people who are focused on the past are standing in the way of progress.

These critics have a point. It's true that resistance to new ideas and nostalgia frequently go hand in hand. That being said, these pundits don't fully understand the relationship between nostalgia and innovation because it is often the case that people who are highly resistant to new ways of doing things are also nostalgic. These people have personalities that make change particularly challenging and anxiety-provoking for them, and therefore they have a strong attachment to order and stability. And because negative psychological states such as anxiety trigger nostalgia, it makes sense that these people would be highly nostalgic, particularly in a fast-changing world. They are living in a world that changes regardless of their preference for stability. This makes them anxious, so they turn to nostalgia for comfort.

Nostalgia does more than provide psychological comfort in a changing world—it helps us become agents of change.

But that doesn't mean that nostalgia is the cause of their resistance to change. Their resistance comes from their personalities and resulting anxiety about change. By providing them comfort in what feels like a chaotic world, nostalgia may actually help them deal with change as best as they can.

These people are probably never going to be champions of bold new ideas, but nostalgia has a soothing effect that can make the change they can't control a little easier to navigate.

It goes without saying that most people aren't this extreme. Sure, some people never want to change, but others are on the polar side of the continuum—they prefer novelty, turnover, and bold risk-taking. But most of us are somewhere between these extremes. For us, nostalgia does more than provide psychological comfort in a changing world—it helps us become agents of change. Nostalgia isn't a barrier to progress; it's a resource for advancing progress.

Nostalgia Drives Progress

In addition to my work in the psychology of nostalgia, I've been developing a new area of research on the psychology of progress. I'm specifically interested in how our current mental states influence our motivation and ability to build a better future.

When people discuss progress, the talk usually focuses on the scientific, technological, political, and legal variables that influence progress. People rarely talk about the impact of psychology, even when it's clear that psychology plays a central role. Progress begins with ideas that are subsequently explored, tested, shared, and debated. Each of these steps relies on psychological processes.

Ideas don't magically transmute themselves into tangible progress all by themselves. People must advocate for them. Influential others must be persuaded. And people must be motivated to advance progress, even when it's difficult or unpleasant. Societal progress starts with a progress mindset. People with a progress mindset are agentic, resilient, inspired, optimistic, and creative. And as I've shown throughout this book, nostalgia supports all these positive psychological states.

Since progress requires experimentation, it inherently involves failure. Imagine if every time a new idea failed, our collective response was to give up. If this were how our minds worked, we'd all still be hunter-gatherers, and not very skilled ones at that, because we'd be resistant to any new attempts to make our hunting and gathering more efficient and successful. Perhaps to some people, this doesn't seem all that bad. As someone who enjoys spending time in nature, I certainly see the benefits of reconnecting with simple, straightforward, and older ways of living. That being said, I also appreciate the scientific, technological, and medical advances that make my life easier, safer, and more comfortable. I think most of us are like this. We're sometimes apprehensive about new changes, but in general we appreciate progress and want it to continue.

We don't want failed attempts at innovation or the damage that's sometimes caused by new ways of doing things to prevent us from pursuing progress as a whole. This means we need to be both agentic and resilient. We need to believe that despite barriers to progress and our failures at trying to solve problems, it's within our power to eventually succeed, and this feeling of agency is what will drive us forward. That agency needs to be coupled with resilience. Failure is difficult. It also happens a lot when we're testing new ideas and exploring fresh possibilities. But we can't let setbacks keep us from trying again. We must persist.

Since nostalgia inspires an agentic and goal-oriented mindset, it can be a vital resource for finding the drive to move forward when things get difficult. When we face setbacks or failures and need to restore our confidence, nostalgia helps by offering a broader perspective as well as reminders of past triumphs. Just like nostalgia can help people who suffer from loneliness or social rejection use past experiences to restore social confidence and motivation, it can help people working on major challenges draw from past successes for inspiration.

To build a better future, people need to envision a better one, and they need to feel motivated to make that vision a reality. When society faces major challenges, it's easy for people to feel hopeless and to see progress as impossible. When people are pessimistic, it's hard for them to find a reason to try to improve things. Instead of looking for ways to go out in the world and make a positive difference, pessimistic people turn inward and can become more self-centered. After all, personal sacrifices don't make sense if the whole thing is pointless. Why not just do your own thing for as long as you can with the maximum amount of enjoyment? But as illustrated in some of the studies I've cited, nostalgia encourages people to become more optimistic.

Nostalgia also inspires creativity, and progress relies on thinking outside the box. One of the reasons progress is often so difficult is because it requires finding new ways of approaching a problem. Creativity leads to innovation. Studies find that people think more creatively after engaging in nostalgic reflection. Looking to the past for inspiration helps open new possibilities for the future.

I think meaning is at the core of a psychology of progress. It's when people believe their lives are meaningful that they are best positioned to adopt a progress mindset, to feel inspired to act with agency and resilience, to go out in the world with an optimistic attitude, and to use creative problem-solving to address the challenges of our time and build a better future.

Again, nostalgia plays a key role in all of this. In our nostalgic memories, we're reminded that life is full of experiences that make it meaningful and that make the world worth improving and humanity worth fighting for. This encourages a more agentic and optimistic mindset. And when we feel more agentic and optimistic, we're more likely to persist, even when it feels near impossible. We are also more inspired to explore new ideas.

Historical and cultural nostalgia may be especially useful for promoting a progress mindset. Individuals and groups working to advance specific causes that could help improve the world (or even just their little corner of it) can nostalgically look to previous stories of progress. When you find yourself thinking that the world is getting worse, that progress is a myth, or that the future is hopeless, it might be useful to look to the past for contrary evidence. People in previous generations made discoveries and sacrifices, created new technologies and medicines, and fought for social and legal changes that people greatly benefit from today. Many of them faced what were widely believed to be impossible or hopeless conditions. We can look to their stories as the types of cultural memories that should be preserved and passed down to future generations.

If nostalgia were just a past-oriented experience, it wouldn't make us feel better about our lives today and more optimistic about our futures.

Nostalgia as a Future-Oriented Experience

I started this book by arguing that humans are progress-oriented by nature. We can certainly be set in our ways and we need a certain amount of stability to thrive. We don't do well in chaos. But we also oppose stagnation. We are curious, explorative, and creative. We like to build and tinker. As much as we're defense-oriented, we're also growth-oriented. We strive for self-improvement.

It seems intuitive to view nostalgia as in opposition to our progress-oriented nature because it involves mental time travel to the past. But it turns out the journey to the past that nostalgia takes us on is really about the present and the future. If nostalgia were just a past-oriented experience, it wouldn't make us feel better about our lives today and more optimistic about our futures. But it does. If nostalgia were merely about the past, it wouldn't inspire us to feel agentic today and motivated to pursue the goals that will improve our lives tomorrow. But it does. If nostalgia were just about how great our lives were when we were younger, it wouldn't inspire us to engage in the prosocial behaviors that will pay dividends in the future. But it does. Nostalgia exists not because we are a past-oriented species but because we are a future-oriented one. When we look for guidance and inspiration to build a better tomorrow, we need our cherished memories. Nostalgia isn't a weakness. It's an undeniable strength.

ACKNOWLEDGMENTS

Writing can often feel like a solitary activity, but authoring a science-based book relies on the work, knowledge, and experience of many other people. I would like to thank my literary agent, Nathaniel Jacks, at Inkwell Management for his ongoing guidance and encouragement. I also want to thank Susan Golant for early editorial assistance. And a big thank you to my editor, Robert Lee, and the whole team at Sounds True for helping me transform my more than two decades of research and consulting on nostalgia into a concise and accessible book that I hope will help many people use their cherished memories to improve their lives and the world around them.

Past Forward draws on research from dozens of outstanding behavioral and social scientists who study nostalgia, motivation, psychological well-being, and physical health, and I am grateful for their work. I would like to thank a few scholars specifically whom I have closely collaborated with on nostalgia research. They include Jamie Arndt, Andrew Abeyta, Jacob Juhl, Taylor FioRito, Matthew Vess, and Jeff Johnson. I especially want to thank my good friends and colleagues Constantine Sedikides and Tim Wildschut, who have done more than anyone to develop the science of nostalgia. I am also very grateful for the encouragement and creative input I have received from my colleagues and friends at Archbridge Institute: Gonzalo Schwarz, Ben Wilterdink, and Kali Keller. I am extremely fortunate to be able to work with such a great team on our shared goal of advancing human flourishing.

Finally, I want to thank my family. My mother, late father, siblings, children, and many others in my extended family have inspired me in distinct and important ways. Most of all, I want to thank my wife, Jenny. Over the last twenty-five years we have shared many adventures and created many nostalgic memories together. This book would not exist without her love and encouragement. *Past Forward* is dedicated to her.

NOTES

Introduction

1. Fyodor Dostoevsky, *The Brothers Karamazov*, trans. and ann. Richard Pevear and Larissa Volokhonsky (San Francisco: North Point Press, 1990).

2. Donald Kraybill, Karen Johnson-Weiner, and Steven Nolt, *The Amish* (Baltimore: Johns Hopkins University Press, 2013).

Chapter 1
The New Science of Nostalgia

1. Johannes Hofer, "Medical Dissertation on Nostalgia," trans. Carolyn Kiser Anspach, *Bulletin of the History of Medicine* 2, no. 6 (1934): 376–91. Original work published 1688.

2. Fred Davis, *Yearning for Yesterday: A Sociology of Nostalgia* (New York: Free Press, 1979), 35–36.

3. Charles Darwin, *The Expression of the Emotions in Man and Animals* (New York: D. Appleton, 1896). Original work published 1872.

4. Davis, *Yearning for Yesterday*.

Chapter 2
Nostalgia Is about the Future

1. *Collins English Dictionary*, Complete and Unabridged 2012 Digital Edition, s.v. "nostalgia," dictionary.com/browse/nostalgia.

2. *Cambridge Dictionary*, s.v. "nostalgia," dictionary.cambridge.org /us/dictionary/english/nostalgia.

3. Erica G. Hepper, Tim Wildschut, Constantine Sedikides, Timothy D. Ritchie, Y.-F. Yung, Nina Hansen, Georgios Abakoumkin, et al., "Pancultural Nostalgia: Prototypical Conceptions across Cultures," *Emotion* 14, no. 4 (August 2014): 733–47, doi:10.1037/a0036790.

4. Xinyue Zhou, Constantine Sedikides, Tiantian Mo, Wanyue Li, Emily K. Hong, and Tim Wildschut, "The Restorative Power of Nostalgia: Thwarting Loneliness by Raising Happiness During the COVID-19 Pandemic," *Social Psychological and Personality Science* 13, no. 4 (2022): 803–15, doi.org/10.1177 /19485506211041830.

Chapter 3
What Makes Nostalgia Possible
(and Necessary)

1. Edward Diener and Mark Walborn, "Effects of Self-Awareness on Anti-Normative Behavior," *Journal of Research in Personality* 10, no. 1 (1976): 107–11.

2. Jamie Ballard, "Half of Americans Say It Should Be Illegal to Burn the US Flag," YouGovAmerica, June 24, 2020, today .yougov.com/topics/politics/articles-reports/2020/06/24/flag -burning-legal-illegal-poll-data.

3. Jeff Greenberg, Jonathan Porteus, Linda Simon, Tom Pyszczynski, and Sheldon Solomon, "Evidence of a Terror Management Function of Cultural Icons: The Effects of Mortality Salience on the Inappropriate Use of Cherished Cultural Symbols," *Personality and Social Psychology Bulletin* 21, no. 11 (1995): 1221–28, doi.org/10.1177/01461672952111010.

4. Mark J. Landau, Brian P. Meier, and Lucas A. Keefer, "A Metaphor-Enriched Social Cognition," *Psychological Bulletin* 136, no. 6 (2010): 1045–67.

5. Adam K. Fetterman, Jacob Juhl, Brian P. Meier, Andrew Abeyta, Clay Routledge, and Michael D. Robinson, "The Path to God Is Through the Heart: Metaphoric Self-Location as a Predictor of Religiosity," *Self & Identity* 19, no. 6 (2020): 650–72.

6. Michael W. Richardson, "How Much Energy Does the Brain Use?," BrainFacts.org, February 1, 2019, brainfacts.org/brain -anatomy-and-function/anatomy/2019/how-much-energy-does -the-brain-use-020119.

7. Tim Wildschut, Constantine Sedikides, Jamie Arndt, and Clay Routledge, "Nostalgia: Content, Triggers, Functions," *Journal of Personality and Social Psychology* 91, no. 5 (2006): 975–93.

Chapter 4
Nostalgia Shapes the Self-Concept

1. American Psychological Association Dictionary of Psychology, s.v. "self," dictionary.apa.org/self.

2. Tim Wildschut, Constantine Sedikides, Jamie Arndt, and Clay Routledge, "Nostalgia: Content, Triggers, Functions," *Journal of Personality and Social Psychology* 91, no. 5 (2006): 975–93.

3. Wildschut, Sedikides, Arndt, and Routledge, "Nostalgia," 975–93.

4. Elena Stephan, Constantine Sedikides, and Tim Wildschut, "Mental Travel into the Past: Differentiating Recollections of Nostalgic, Ordinary, and Positive Events," *European Journal of Social Psychology* 42, no. 3 (2012): 290–98.

5. Alison P. Lenton, Martin Bruder, Letitia Gabriela Slabu, and Constantine Sedikides, "How Does 'Being Real' Feel? The Experience of State Authenticity," *Journal of Personality* 81, no. 3 (2013): 276–89.

6. Matthew Baldwin, Monica Biernat, and Mark J. Landau, "Remembering the Real Me: Nostalgia Offers a Window to the Intrinsic Self," *Journal of Personality and Social Psychology* 108, no. 1 (2015): 128–47.

7. Baldwin, Biernat, and Landau, "Remembering the Real Me," 128–47.

8. Michael Chandler and Travis Proulx, "Changing Selves in Changing Worlds: Youth Suicide on the Fault-Lines of Colliding Cultures," *Archives of Suicide Research* 10, no. 2 (2006): 125–40.

9. Fred Davis, *Yearning for Yesterday: A Sociology of Nostalgia* (New York: Free Press, 1979), 35–36.

10. Constantine Sedikides, Tim Wildschut, Clay Routledge, and Jamie Arndt, "Nostalgia Counteracts Self-Discontinuity and Restores Self-Continuity," *European Journal of Social Psychology* 45, no. 1 (2015): 52–61.

11. Sedikides, Wildschut, Routledge, and Arndt, "Nostalgia Counteracts Self-Discontinuity," 52–61.

12. Sedikides, Wildschut, Routledge, and Arndt, 52–61.

13. Constantine Sedikides, Tim Wildschut, W. Y. Cheung, Clay Routledge, Erica Hepper, Jamie Arndt, Kenneth Vail, et al., "Nostalgia Fosters Self-Continuity: Uncovering the Mechanism (Social Connectedness) and Consequence (Eudaimonic Well-Being)," *Emotion* 16, no. 4 (2016): 524–39.

14. Sanda Ismail, Gary Christopher, Emily Dodd, Tim Wildschut, Constantine Sedikides, Thomas Ingram, Roy Jones, et al., "Psychological and Mnemonic Benefits of Nostalgia for People with Dementia," *Journal of Alzheimer's Disease* 65, no. 4 (2018): 1327–44.

Chapter 5
Nostalgia Builds Healthy Self-Esteem

1. Will Storr, *Selfie: How We Became So Self-Obsessed and What It's Doing to Us* (London: Picador, 2017).

2. Constantine Sedikides, Lowell Gaertner, and Yoshiyasu Toguchi, "Pancultural Self-Enhancement," *Journal of Personality and Social Psychology* 84, no. 1 (2003): 60–79.

3. Tim Wildschut, Constantine Sedikides, Jamie Arndt, and Clay Routledge, "Nostalgia: Content, Triggers, Functions," *Journal of Personality and Social Psychology* 91, no. 5 (2006): 975–93.

4. Elena Stephan, Constantine Sedikides, Tim Wildschut, W. Y. Cheung, Clay Routledge, and Jamie Arndt, "Nostalgia-Evoked Inspiration: Mediating Mechanisms and Motivational Implications," *Personality and Social Psychology Bulletin* 4, no. 10 (2015): 1395–1410.

5. Clay Routledge, Jamie Arndt, and Jamie L. Goldenberg, "A Time to Tan: Proximal and Distal Effects of Mortality Salience on Sun Exposure Intentions," *Personality and Social Psychology Bulletin* 30, no. 10 (2004): 1347–58.

6. Ben-Ari Orit Taubman, Victor Florian, and Mario Mikulincer, "The Impact of Mortality Salience on Reckless Driving: A Test of Terror Management Mechanisms," *Journal of Personality and Social Psychology* 76, no. 1 (1999): 35–45.

7. Alex Cook, "Coins, Toys and Trading Cards: 83% of Collectors Think Their Collection Will Pay Off," Magnify Money, updated April 11, 2022, magnifymoney.com/news/collectors-survey/.

8. Matthew Vess, Jamie Arndt, Clay Routledge, Constantine Sedikides, and Tim Wildschut, "Nostalgia as a Resource for the Self," *Self and Identity* 11, no. 3, (2012): 273–84, doi:10.1080/15298868.2010.521452.

Chapter 6
Nostalgia Helps the Self
Grow and Expand

1. Jeff Greenberg, Sheldon Solomon, Tom Pyszczynski, Abram Rosenblatt, John Burling, Deborah Lyon, Linda Simon, and Elizabeth Pinel, "Why Do People Need Self-Esteem? Converging Evidence That Self-Esteem Serves an Anxiety-Buffering Function," *Journal of Personality and Social Psychology* 63, no. 6 (1992): 913–22.

2. Kennon M. Sheldon and Andrew J. Elliot, "Goal Striving, Need Satisfaction, and Longitudinal Well-Being: The Self-Concordance Model," *Journal of Personality and Social Psychology* 76, no. 3 (1999): 482–97.

3. Dymphna C. van den Boom, "The Influence of Temperament and Mothering on Attachment and Exploration: An Experimental Manipulation of Sensitive Responsiveness among Lower Class Mothers with Irritable Infants," *Child Development* 65, no. 5 (1994): 1457–77.

4. Holly H. Schiffrin, Miriam Liss, Haley Miles-McLean, Katherine A. Geary, Mindy J. Erchull, and Taryn Tashner, "Helping or Hovering? The Effects of Helicopter Parenting on College Students' Well-Being," *Journal of Child and Family Studies* 23, no. 3 (2014): 548–57.

5. Constantine Sedikides, Tim Wildschut, Clay Routledge, Jamie Arndt, Erica Hepper, and Xinyue Zhou, "To Nostalgize: Mixing Memory with Affect and Desire," *Advances in Experimental Social Psychology* 51, no. 1 (2015): 189–258.

6. Taylor A. FioRito and Clay Routledge, "Is Nostalgia a Past or Future-Focused Experience? Affective, Behavioral, Social Cognitive, and Neuroscientific Evidence," *Frontiers in Psychology* 11 (2020), frontiersin.org/articles/10.3389/fpsyg.2020.01133/full.

7. Shengquan Ye, Rose Ying Lam Ngan, and Anna N. N. Hui, "The State, Not the Trait, of Nostalgia Increases Creativity," *Creativity Research Journal* 25, no. 3 (2013): 317–23.

8. Wijnand A. P. van Tilburg, Constantine Sedikides, and Tim Wildschut, "The Mnemonic Muse: Nostalgia Fosters Creativity Through Openness to Experience," *Journal of Experimental Social Psychology* 59 (2015): 1–7.

9. Tilburg, Sedikides, and Wildschut, "Mnemonic Muse," 1–7.

Chapter 7
Nostalgia Strengthens and
Builds Relationships

1. Peter Walker, "May Appoints Minister to Tackle Loneliness Issues Raised by Jo Cox," *The Guardian*, January 16, 2018, theguardian.com/society/2018/jan/16/may-appoints-minister -tackle-loneliness-issues-raised-jo-cox.

2. Colleen Walsh, "Young Adults Hardest Hit by Loneliness During the Pandemic," *Harvard Gazette*, February 17, 2021, news.harvard.edu/gazette/story/2021/02/young-adults-teens -loneliness-mental-health-coronavirus-covid-pandemic/.

3. Daniel A. Cox, "The State of American Friendship: Change, Challenges, and Loss," Survey Center on American Life, June 8, 2021, americansurveycenter.org/research/the-state-of-american -friendship-change-challenges-and-loss/.

4. Jean M. Twenge, "Have Smartphones Destroyed a Generation?," *The Atlantic*, September 2017, theatlantic.com/magazine/archive /2017/09/has-the-smartphone-destroyed-a-generation/534198/.

5. Jamie Ballard, "Millennials Are the Loneliest Generation," YouGovAmerica, July 30, 2019, today. yougov.com/topics/society/articles-reports/2019/07/30/ loneliness-friendship-new-friends-poll-survey.

6. Louise C. Hawkley and John T. Cacioppo, "Loneliness Matters: A Theoretical and Empirical Review of Consequences and Mechanisms," *Annals of Behavioral Medicine* 40, no. 2 (2010): 218–27.

7. Julianne Holt-Lunstad, Timothy B. Smith, Mark Baker, Tyler Harris, and David Stephenson, "Loneliness and Social Isolation as Risk Factors for Mortality: A Meta-Analytic Review," *Perspectives on Psychological Science* 10, no. 2 (2015): 227–37.

8. Tim Wildschut, Constantine Sedikides, Jamie Arndt, and Clay Routledge, "Nostalgia: Content, Triggers, Functions," *Journal of Personality and Social Psychology* 91, no. 5 (2006): 975–93.

9. Xinyue Zhou, Constantine Sedikides, Tim Wildschut, and Ding-Guo Gao, "Counteracting Loneliness: On the Restorative Function of Nostalgia," *Psychological Science* 19, no. 10 (2008): 1023–29.

10. Constantine Sedikides, Tim Wildschut, Jamie Arndt, and Clay Routledge, "Nostalgia: Past, Present, and Future," *Current Directions in Psychological Science* 17, no. 5 (2008): 304–7.

11. Andrew A. Abeyta, Clay Routledge, and Jacob Juhl, "Looking Back to Move Forward: Nostalgia as a Psychological Resource for Promoting Relationship Aspirations and Overcoming Relationship Challenges," *Journal of Personality and Social Psychology* 109, no. 6 (2015): 1029–44.

12. Wildschut, Sedikides, Arndt, and Routledge, "Nostalgia," 975–93.

13. Clay Routledge, Tim Wildschut, Constantine Sedikides, and Jacob Juhl, "Nostalgia as a Resource for Psychological Health and Well-Being," *Social and Personality Psychology Compass* 7, no. 11 (2013): 808–18.

14. Abeyta, Routledge, and Juhl, "Looking Back to Move Forward," 1029–44.

15. Zhou, Sedikides, Wildschut, and Gao, "Counteracting Loneliness," 1023–29.

16. Xinyue Zhou, Constantinne Sedikides, Tiantian Mo, Wanyue Li, Emily Hong, and Tim Wildschut, "The Restorative Power of Nostalgia: Thwarting Loneliness by Raising Happiness During the COVID-19 Pandemic," *Social Psychological and Personality Science* 13, no. 4 (2022): 803–15.

17. Rogelio Puente-Diaz and Judith Cavazos-Arroyo, "Fighting Social Isolation with Nostalgia: Nostalgia as a Resource for Feeling Connected and Appreciated and Instilling Optimism and Vitality During the COVID-19 Pandemic," *Frontiers in Psychology* 12 (2021), frontiersin.org/articles/10.3389 /fpsyg.2021.740247/full.

18. Chelsea A. Reid, Jeffrey D. Green, Tim Wildschut, and Constantine Sedikides, "Scent-Evoked Nostalgia," *Memory* 23, no. 2 (2015): 157–66.

19. Taylor A. FioRito and Clay Routledge, "Is Nostalgia a Past or Future-Focused Experience? Affective, Behavioral, Social Cognitive, and Neuroscientific Evidence," *Frontiers in Psychology* 11 (2020), frontiersin.org/articles/10.3389/fpsyg .2020.01133/full.

20. Andrew A. Abeyta, Clay Routledge, and Jacob Juhl, "Looking Back to Move Forward: Nostalgia as a Psychological Resource for Promoting Relationship Aspirations and Overcoming Relationship Challenges," *Journal of Personality and Social Psychology* 109, no. 6 (2015): 1029–44.

21. Abeyta, Routledge, and Juhl, "Looking Back to Move Forward," 1029–44.

22. Constantine Sedikides and Tim Wildschut, "The Motivational Potency of Nostalgia: The Future Is Called Yesterday," *Advances in Motivation Science* 7 (2020): 75–111.

23. Abeyta, Routledge, and Juhl, "Looking Back to Move Forward," 1029–44.

24. Elena Stephan, Tim Wildschut, Constantine Sedikides, Xinyue Zhou, Wuming He, Clay Routledge, Wing-Yee Cheung, and Ad J. J. M. Vingerhoets, "The Mnemonic Mover: Nostalgia Regulates Avoidance and Approach Motivation," *Emotion* 14, no. 3 (2014): 545–61.

Chapter 8
Nostalgia Connects You to Groups

1. Tim Wildschut, Martin Bruder, Sara Robertson, Wijnand A. P. van Tilburg, and Constantine Sedikides, "Collective Nostalgia: A Group-Level Emotion That Confers Unique Benefits on the Group," *Journal of Personality and Social Psychology* 107, no. 5 (2014): 844–63.

2. Wildschut, Bruder, Robertson, van Tilburg, and Sedikides, "Collective Nostalgia," 844–63.

3. Jeffrey D. Green, Athena H. Cairo, Tim Wildschut, and Constantine Sedikides, "The Ties That Bind: University Nostalgia Fosters Relational and Collective University Engagement," *Frontiers in Psychology* 11 (2021): 580731.

4. Alex Nowrasteh and Andrew C. Forrester, "Immigrants Recognize American Greatness: Immigrants and Their Descendants Are Patriotic and Trust America's Governing Institutions," Cato Institute, February 4, 2019, cato.org /publications/immigration-research-policy-brief/immigrants -recognize-american-greatness-immigrants.

5. Clay Routledge, "Who Is Proud to Be American?," Archbridge Institute and Sheila and Robert Challey Institute for Global Innovation and Growth, December 2020, archbridgeinstitute. org/wpcontent/uploads/2020/12/Archbridge_ ProudtobeAmerican_Routledge.pdf.

6. Wildschut, Bruder, Robertson, van Tilburg, and Sedikides, "Collective Nostalgia," 844–63.

7. Department of State, *Report to Congress Pursuant to Section 5 of the Elie Wiesel Genocide and Atrocities Prevention Act of 2018*, P.L. 115-441, state.gov/wp-content/uploads/2021/07/uilwmf3mj.pdf.

8. *Britannica*, s.v. "Henri Tajfel," last updated April 29, 2023, britannica.com/biography/Henri-Tajfel.

9. Henri Tajfel and John C. Turner, "The Social Identity Theory of Intergroup Behaviour," in *Psychology of Intergroup Relations*, ed. Stephen Worchel and William G. Austin (Chicago: Nelson-Hall, 1986), 7–24.

10. Anouk Smeekes, Constantine Sedikides, and Tim Wildschut, "Collective Nostalgia: Triggers and Consequences for Collective Action," *British Journal of Social Psychology* 62, no. 1 (2023): 197–214.

Chapter 9
Nostalgia Helps You Care about Others

1. C. Nathan DeWall and Roy F. Baumeister, "Alone But Feeling No Pain: Effects of Social Exclusion on Physical Pain Tolerance and Pain Threshold, Affective Forecasting, and Interpersonal Empathy," *Journal of Personality and Social Psychology* 91, no. 1 (2006): 1–15.

2. Jean M. Twenge, Roy F. Baumeister, C. Nathan DeWall, Natalie J. Ciarocco, and J. Michael Bartels, "Social Exclusion Decreases Prosocial Behavior," *Journal of Personality and Social Psychology* 92, no. 1 (2007): 56.

3. Jean M. Twenge, Roy F. Baumeister, Dianne M. Tice, and Tanja S. Stucke, "If You Can't Join Them, Beat Them: Effects of Social Exclusion on Aggressive Behavior," *Journal of Personality and Social Psychology* 81, no. 6 (2001): 1058–69.

4. Frode Stenseng, Jay Belsky, Vera Skalicka, and Lars Wichstrøm, "Preschool Social Exclusion, Aggression, and Cooperation: A Longitudinal Evaluation of the Need-to-Belong and the Social-Reconnection Hypotheses," *Personality and Social Psychology Bulletin* 40, no. 12 (2014): 1637–47.

5. Jean M. Twenge, Liqing Zhang, Kathleen R. Catanese, Brenda Dolan-Pascoe, Leif F. Lyche, and Roy F. Baumeister, "Replenishing Connectedness: Reminders of Social Activity Reduce Aggression After Social Exclusion," pt. 1, *British Journal of Social Psychology* 46 (2007): 205–24.

6. Dennis T. Regan, "Effects of a Favor and Liking on Compliance," *Journal of Experimental Social Psychology* 7, no. 6 (1971): 627–39; R. Matthew Montoya and Robert S. Horton, "The Reciprocity of Liking Effect," in *The Psychology of Love*, ed. Michele A. Paludi (Santa Barbara, CA: Praeger, 2012), 39–57.

7. Kathi L. Tidd and Joan S. Lockard, "Monetary Significance of the Affiliative Smile: A Case for Reciprocal Altruism," *Bulletin of the Psychonomic Society* 11, no. 6 (1978): 344–46.

8. Kerry Breen, "Over 900 Cars Paid for Each Others' Meals at This Dairy Queen Drive-Thru," Today, December 10, 2020, today.com/food/over-900-cars-paid-each-other-s-meals-dairy-queen-t203616.

9. Robert A. Emmons, Jeffrey Froh, and Rachel Rose, "Gratitude," in *Positive Psychological Assessment: A Handbook of Models and Measures*, ed. Matthew W. Gallagher and Shane J. Lopez (Washington, DC: American Psychological Association, 2019), 317–32.

10. Robert A. Emmons and Robin Stern, "Gratitude as a Psychotherapeutic Intervention," *Journal of Clinical Psychology* 69, no. 8 (2013): 846–55.

11. Sara B. Algoe, Shelly L. Gable, and Natalya C. Maisel, "It's the Little Things: Everyday Gratitude as a Booster Shot for Romantic Relationships," *Personal Relationships* 17, no. 2 (2010): 217–33; C. Nathan DeWall, Nathaniel M. Lambert, Richard S. Pond Jr., Todd P. Kashdan, and Frank D. Fincham, "A Grateful Heart Is a Nonviolent Heart: Cross-Sectional, Experience Sampling, Longitudinal, and Experimental Evidence," *Social Psychological and Personality Science* 3, no. 2 (2012): 232–40; Monica Y. Bartlett and David DeSteno, "Gratitude and Prosocial Behavior: Helping When It Costs You," *Psychological Science* 17, no. 4 (2006): 319–25.

12. Xinyue Zhou, Tim Wildschut, Constantine Sedikides, Kan Shi, and Cong Feng, "Nostalgia: The Gift That Keeps On Giving," *Journal of Consumer Research* 39, no. 1 (2012): 39–50.

13. Zhou, Wildschut, Sedikides, Shi, and Cong Feng, "Nostalgia," 39–50.

14. Zhou, Wildschut, Sedikides, Shi, and Cong Feng, 39–50.

15. Elena Stephan, Tim Wildschut, Constantine Sedikides, Xinyue Zhou, Wuming He, Clay Routledge, Wing-Yee Cheung, and Ad J. J. M. Vingerhoets, "The Mnemonic Mover: Nostalgia Regulates Avoidance and Approach Motivation," *Emotion* 14, no. 3 (2014): 545–61.

16. Jacob Juhl, Tim Wildschut, Constantine Sedikides, Xiling Xiong, and Xinyue Zhou, "Nostalgia Promotes Help Seeking by Fostering Social Connectedness," *Emotion* 21, no. 3 (2021): 631–43.

17. Juhl, Wildschut, Sedikides, Xiong, and Zhou, "Nostalgia Promotes Help Seeking," 631–43.

Chapter 10
Nostalgia Helps You Cope with Existential Fears

1. Ernest Becker, *The Denial of Death* (New York: Free Press, 1973).

2. Clay Routledge and Matthew Vess, eds., *The Handbook of Terror Management Theory* (New York: Elsevier, 2018).

3. Clay Routledge, Jamie Arndt, Constantine Sedikides, and Tim Wildschut, "A Blast from the Past: The Terror Management Function of Nostalgia," *Journal of Experimental Social Psychology* 44, no. 1 (2008): 132–40; Jacob Juhl, Clay Routledge, Jamie Arndt, Constantine Sedikides, and Tim Wildschut, "Fighting the Future with the Past: Nostalgia Buffers Existential Threat," *Journal of Research in Personality* 44, no. 3 (2010): 309–14.

4. Juhl, Routledge, Arndt, Sedikides, and Wildschut, "Fighting the Future with the Past," 309–14.

5. W. Dewi Rees, "The Hallucinations of Widowhood," *British Medical Journal* 4, no. 5778 (1971): 37–41.

6. P. Richard Olson, Joe A. Suddeth, Patricia J. Peterson, and Claudia Egelhoff, "Hallucinations of Widowhood," *Journal of the American Geriatrics Society* 33, no. 8 (1985): 543–47.

7. Marios Biskas, Jacob Juhl, Tim Wildschut, Constantine Sedikides, and Vassilis Saroglou, "Nostalgia and Spirituality: The Roles of Self-Continuity and Meaning in Life," *Social Psychology* 53, no. 3 (2022): 152–62.

8. Mike Morrison and Neal J. Roese, "Regrets of the Typical American: Findings from a Nationally Representative Sample," *Social Psychological and Personality Science* 2, no. 6 (2011): 576–83.

9. Anna Kleinspehn-Ammerlahn, Dana Krotter-Grühn, and Jacqui Smith, "Self-Perceptions of Aging: Do Subjective Age and Satisfaction with Aging Change During Old Age?," *Journal of Gerontology: Psychological Sciences* 63, no. 6 (2008): 377–85.

10. Sonja Boehmer, "Relationships Between Felt Age and Perceived Disability, Satisfaction with Recovery, Self-Efficacy Beliefs, and Coping Strategies," *Journal of Health Psychology* 12, no. 6 (2007): 895–906.

11. Yannick Stephan, Angela R. Sutin, and Antonio Terracciano, "Younger Subjective Age Is Associated with Lower C-Reactive Protein among Older Adults," *Brain, Behavior, and Immunity* 43 (2015): 33–36.

12. Dana Krotter-Grühn, Anna Kleinspehn-Ammerlahn, Denis Gerstorf, and Jacqui Smith, "Self-Perceptions of Aging Predict Mortality and Change with Approaching Death: 16-Year Longitudinal Results from the Berlin Aging Study," *Psychology and Aging* 24, no. 3 (2009): 654–67.

13. Yannick Stephan, Aïna Chalabaev, Dana Krotter-Grühn, and Alban Jaconelli, "Feeling Younger, Being Stronger': An Experimental Study of Subjective Age and Physical Functioning Among Older Adults," *Journals of Gerontology, Series B: Psychological and Social Sciences* 68, no. 1 (2013): 1–7.

14. Andrew A. Abeyta and Clay Routledge, "Fountain of Youth: The Impact of Nostalgia on Youthfulness and Implications for Health," *Self & Identity* 15, no. 3 (2016): 356–69.

15. Abeyta and Routledge, "Fountain of Youth," 356–69.

16. Abeyta and Routledge, 356–69.

Chapter 11
Nostalgia Focuses You on What
Gives You Meaning

1. Stephanie A. Hooker and Kevin S. Masters, "Daily Meaning Salience and Physical Activity in Previously Inactive Exercise Initiates," *Health Psychology* 37, no. 4 (2018): 344–54.

2. Taylor A. Nelson, Andrew A. Abeyta, and Clay Routledge, "What Makes Life Meaningful for Theists and Atheists?," *Psychology of Religion and Spirituality* 13, no. 1 (2021): 111–18.

3. Laura Silver, Patrick van Kessel, Christine Huang, Laura Clancy, and Sneha Gubbala, "What Makes Life Meaningful? Views from 17 Advanced Economies," Pew Research Center, November 18, 2021, pewresearch.org/global/2021/11/18/what-makes-life-meaningful-views-from-17-advanced-economies/.

4. Nathaniel M. Lambert, Tyler F. Stillman, Joshua A. Hicks, Shanmukh Kamble, Roy F. Baumeister, and Frank D. Fincham, "To Belong Is to Matter: Sense of Belonging Enhances Meaning in Life," *Personality and Social Psychology Bulletin* 39, no. 11 (2013): 1418–27.

5. S. Katherine Nelson, Kostadin Kushlev, Tammy English, Elizabeth W. Dunn, and Sonja Lyubomirsky, "In Defense of Parenthood: Children Are Associated with More Joy Than Misery," *Psychological Science* 24, no. 1 (2013): 3–10.

6. Clay Routledge, Jamie Arndt, Tim Wildschut, Constantine Sedikides, Claire M. Hart, Jacob Juhl, Ad J. J. M. Vingerhoets, and Wolff Scholtz, "The Past Makes the Present Meaningful: Nostalgia as an Existential Resource," *Journal of Personality and Social Psychology* 101, no. 3 (2011): 638–52.

7. Paul J. Maher, Eric R. Igou, and Wijnand A. P. van Tilburg, "Nostalgia Relieves the Disillusioned Mind," *Journal of Experimental Psychology* 92 (2021): 104061.

8. Eric R. Igou and Wijnand A. P. van Tilburg, "The Existential Sting of Boredom: Implications for Moral Judgments and Behavior," in *The Moral Psychology of Boredom*, ed. Andreas Elpidorou (Lanham, MD: Rowman & Littlefield, 2021).

9. Wijnand A. P. van Tilburg, Eric R. Igou, and Constantine Sedikides, "In Search of Meaningfulness: Nostalgia as an Antidote to Boredom," *Emotion* 13, no. 3 (2013): 450–61.

10. Clay Routledge, Constantine Sedikides, Tim Wildschut, and Jacob Juhl, "Finding Meaning in One's Past: Nostalgia as an Existential Resource," in *The Psychology of Meaning*, ed. Kenneth D. Markman, Travis Proulx, and Matthew J. Lindberg (Washington, DC: American Psychological Association, 2013), 297–316; Jacob Juhl and Clay Routledge, "Nostalgia Bolsters Perceptions of a Meaningful Self in a Meaningful World," in *The Experience of Meaning in Life: Perspectives from the Psychological Sciences*, ed. Joshua Hicks and Clay Routledge (New York: Springer Press, 2013), 213–26.

11. Constantine Sedikides and Tim Wildschut, "Finding Meaning in Nostalgia," *Review of General Psychology* 22, no. 1 (2018): 48–61.

12. Van Tilburg, Igou, and Sedikides, "In Search of Meaningfulness," 450–61.

Chapter 12
Nostalgia Inspires
Existential Agency

1. Viktor E. Frankl, *Man's Search for Meaning: An Introduction to Logotherapy* (Boston: Beacon Press, 1962).

2. Constantine Sedikides, Wing-Yee Cheung, Tim Wildschut, Erica Hepper, Einar Baldursson, and Bendt Pedersen, "Nostalgia Motivates Pursuit of Important Goals by Increasing Meaning in Life," *European Journal of Social Psychology* 48, no. 2 (2018): 209–16.

3. Nicolas Gueaguen, "The Effects of a Joke on Tipping When It Is Delivered at the Same Time as the Bill," *Journal of Applied Social Psychology* 32, no. 9 (2002): 1955–63.

4. Peggy A. Thoits and Lyndi N. Hewitt, "Volunteer Work and Well-Being," *Journal of Health and Social Behavior* 42, no. 2 (2001): 115–31.

Chapter 13
Nostalgia Helps You Navigate
a Fast-Moving World

1. Melinda J. Milligan, "Displacement and Identity Discontinuity: The Role of Nostalgia in Establishing New Identity Categories," *Symbolic Interaction* 26, no. 3 (2003): 381–403.

2. Niwen Huang, Shijiang Zuo, Fang Wang, Yawen Li, Pan Cai, and Shun Wang, "New Technology Evokes Old Memories: Frequent Smartphone Use Increases Feeling of Nostalgia," *Personality and Social Psychology Bulletin* 49, no. 1 (2023): 138–51.

3. "The New Normal: Phone Use Is Up Nearly 4-Fold Since 2019, According to Tech Care Company Asurion," Asurion, asurion.com/connect/news/tech-usage/.

4. Shalini Misra, Lulu Cheng, Jamie Genevie, and Miao Yuan, "The iPhone Effect: The Quality of In-Person Social Interactions in the Presence of Mobile Devices," *Environment and Behavior* 48, no. 2 (2016): 275–98.

5. Rhiannon N. Turner, Tim Wildschut, and Constantine Sedikides, "Fighting Ageism Through Nostalgia," *European Journal of Social Psychology* 48, no. 2 (2018): 196–208.

6. Rhiannon N. Turner, Tim Wildschut, Constantine Sedikides, and Mirona Gheorghiu, "Combating the Mental Health Stigma with Nostalgia," *European Journal of Social Psychology* 43, no. 5 (2013): 413–22.

ABOUT THE AUTHOR

Dr. Clay Routledge is a leading expert in existential psychology. His work focuses on helping people reach their full potential and build meaningful lives. Clay is vice president of research and director of the Human Flourishing Lab at Archbridge Institute. Prior to joining Archbridge Institute, Clay spent two decades in academia as a professor of psychology, professor of management, and distinguished professor of business. During that time, he taught undergraduate, MBA, and PhD courses in social and personality psychology, cultural psychology, research methods, organizational behavior, and team leadership. Clay is the author of *Nostalgia: A Psychological Resource* and *Supernatural: Death, Meaning, and the Power of the Invisible World*. He has also authored articles for many popular media outlets including the *New York Times*, the *Wall Street Journal*, *USA Today*, *Newsweek*, *Fortune*, *Entrepreneur*, and *Harvard Business Review*. Clay lives with his wife, Jenny, and their dog, Pixie, in Northwest Arkansas. For more, please visit clayroutledge.com

ABOUT SOUNDS TRUE

Sounds True was founded in 1985 by Tami Simon with a clear mission: to disseminate spiritual wisdom. Since starting out as a project with one woman and her tape recorder, we have grown into a multimedia publishing company with a catalog of more than 3,000 titles by some of the leading teachers and visionaries of our time, and an ever-expanding family of beloved customers from across the world.

In more than three decades of evolution, Sounds True has maintained our focus on our overriding purpose and mission: to wake up the world. We offer books, audio programs, online learning experiences, and in-person events to support your personal growth and awakening, and to unlock our greatest human capacities to love and serve.

At SoundsTrue.com you'll find a wealth of resources to enrich your journey, including our weekly *Insights at the Edge* podcast, free downloads, and information about our nonprofit Sounds True Foundation, where we strive to remove financial barriers to the materials we publish through scholarships and donations worldwide.

To learn more, please visit SoundsTrue.com/freegifts or call us toll-free at 800.333.9185.

Together, we can wake up the world.

Ethno (culture) graphy (the process of writing, representing, recording, describing): a field of study

AutoEthnography: qualitative research using self-reflection and writing to explore personal experience and connect this autobiographical story to wider cultural and social meanings and understandings